The Jeshua Code

Secret Teachings from
Jeshua ben Joseph

By
James F. Twyman

<u>Enlightenment Partnership Program</u>

Imagine having James Twyman walk you straight into Heaven. The Enlightenment Partnership Program gives you direct, personal, one on one contact with James every day for three months. Each day you'll exchange texts and emails, and once a week you and James will share a private Zoom call. If you want to take the final step into the experience of nonduality, this may be the perfect program.

You can schedule a 10 minute phone call with James to see if this is the right step for you. Go to <u>www.JamesFTwyman.com</u> and set a time for your private call.

Books by James F. Twyman

The Moses Code

The Art of Spiritual Peacemaking

The Barn Dance

Emissary of Light

Emissary of Love

Giovanni and the Camino of St. Francis

I AM Wishes Fulfilled Meditation
(with Dr. Wayne Dyer)

The Kabbalah Code: A True Adventure
(with Philip Gruber)

Love, God, and the Art of French Cooking

Messages From Thomas

The Prayer of St. Francis

Praying Peace

The Proof
(with Anakha Coman)

The Proposing Tree

St. Francis and the Animals Who Loved Him

The Secret of the Beloved Disciple

Ten Spiritual Lessons I Learned at the Mall

Touching the Divine

The Impersonal Light: Journey into I AM Consciousness

The Nondual Universe — The Spirituality of
Enlightenment Made Simple for the Western World

ISBN: **ISBN:** 9798841662303 (paperback)

Table of Contents

Forward To The New Edition

Nineteen years ago, in 2002, the world I thought I knew shook beneath my feet. I was floating in a hot spring beside the Dead Sea when I looked up and saw a young man looking down at me. He was dressed in white and at first I thought he was just another Israeli getting ready to slip into the mineral water. I think I actually moved to the side to let him in, but when I looked up something about his eyes caught my attention. They were shining like the sun and I'll never forget the feeling in my heart at that moment. It was stirring — that's the clearest I can put it — stirring in a way I had never experienced before. Then he smiled, and a conversation began that has since touched the lives of thousands of people.

As you're about to discover, the man I saw staring down at me was Jeshua. Maybe you call him Jesus, but that never felt quite right to me. This wasn't the Jesus found in classic literature, paintings or sculpted by the great artists of the world. This was the same man who walked the paths I had been walking since I arrived in Israel, and the adventure he led me on was probably not much different than the journey he took with his closest disciples two thousand years ago.

i

It was a journey into the great mystery of awakening, enlightenment and remembering that we're one with God and all creation this and every moment. It has taken me all these years to fully unwrap that experience, and I think I'm finally ready. That's why I decided to re-release this book nearly 20 years after that fateful moment when I first looked into those amazing eyes.

I have to be honest, it wasn't actually my idea. Earlier this afternoon I received an email from a man named Paul asking if there was a paperback version of the book available. He shared the deep impact The Art of Spiritual Peacemaking (the original title) had on his life and he wanted to buy copies for everyone he knew. I explained that it had only been released in hardcover but that it hadn't been in print for many years.

"It should be a bestseller," he said. "Everyone needs to read this. Maybe if you rebranded it as The Jeshua Code."

It was as if a bright light suddenly switched on inside my mind. He was right. *Everyone needs to read this book*, I thought, not because of me, but because the experience I had with Jeshua was real and the information he shared was critically important, now more than ever. He said that he would place a code at the center of each lesson, one the intellectual mind would never comprehend but which the soul would immediately recognize.

"It's like a key slipping into a lock," he once said. "When the right combination of grooves match the inner workings of the lock, the tumblers fall into place on their own and the door opens."

A door had opened in Paul's mind, and the same door was beginning to swing open in my own. After so many years!

There are thirty-three original lessons contained in this volume, and they're being shared here exactly as I received them, word for word. This was stressed over and over by Jeshua.

"Don't do any editing," he said. "Whenever you're ready to write a lesson get into hot water, a bathtub or a hot tub, then wait for me. You'll know when I'm there. It might feel like a clicking sensation deep within your mind. Then get out as quickly as you can and start writing, or typing, and most of all DON'T THINK. Write until you feel me stop you. If you follow these instructions perfectly, the code will be in place."

I did exactly as he instructed. Whenever I felt the sensation he described, I looked down at the word count. As you'll read in the introduction I wrote in

2005, eighty percent of the time there were exactly 999 words. Most of all, I could feel a powerful vibration when I went back to read what I had written, and I feel it again as I'm going through it now. I believe, just as I have always believed, that the wisdom found in these lessons are the original teachings of Jeshua, the lessons he couldn't teach to the masses but which are so important today.

In the original version of this book published in 2006 I included 365 shorter lessons meant for daily reflection. I decided that in The Jeshua Code version I would hold those lessons for a later volume and let the original thirty-three stand on their own. This is the real heart of everything Jeshua shared, and I want to honor that. Also, you'll notice that at the end of each lesson the word Brother appears. This is how the Christ presents Itself here, not as one who is above and beyond the rest of us, but as one who is intimately linked with everything we experience. Perhaps it was also a way to identify the energy I shared with Jeshua as we wrote the lessons. We are brothers, just as we are all brothers and sisters to each other, and the familial energy we share is the essence of the code we are being offered here.

I hope you discover a deep well of wisdom and transformation in these pages. All I know is that if you give yourself to them without reserve, they will give everything back to you.

July 7, 2022

Namaste Village, Ajijic, Mexico

Introduction

Three events led to the composition of this book, or should I say the translation of this material. On one hand, I'm not quick to claim that this is a work of channeling, primarily because I tend to disagree with the common understanding of the phenomenon. More about that later.

Yet, I'm also fully aware that most of the information in this collections did not come from my own conscious mind. Even today I read them and am amazed at their insightfulness, depth, and profundity. In fact, if I were to choose two or three books that I would take with me to a desert island, this would be one of them. That doesn't mean I like reading my own words; rather, there is something I find within these words that I've only discovered a handful of other times in my life. What I discovered is Truth, pure and simple, and that is something to acknowledge and honor, whatever the source. The lessons in this volume came "from" me and they came "through" me. Both seem to be true and, as I have recently learned, in the end they are the same.

Let me begin by describing the second of the three events that led to my writing, or perhaps scribing, this text. In 2003 I had the privilege of leading a group of about 65 pilgrims to the Holy Land, a journey I had made three other times on my own. I discovered a phenomenon there that probably doesn't exist anywhere else in the world, a presence or palpable energy that radiates out in every direction, and it doesn't take an intuitive to feel it. Perhaps it comes from the many prophets and saviors who walked that sacred ground for so many centuries, or perhaps it's due to an event that has yet come to pass. All I know is that the ground seems to vibrate with the spiritual energy which great prophets, from Abraham to Jesus to Muhammad, left in their wake.

Jerusalem itself is the most sacred city in the world to Jews and Christians, and the second most sacred city to Muslims. It's like Disney World to devout seekers, whether they be "religious" or simply "spiritual." On the other hand, the Holy Land is one of the most troubled areas in the world, as it has been for over two thousand years. It is a wonder, then, that Jerusalem, a city whose name translates to "City of Peace," is viewed by many as ground zero for the New World where cooperation and inclusion finally prevail. Perhaps the thinking is, "If they can get it right there, the rest will be easy." These are the main reasons I believe modern Spiritual Peacemakers need to come here, because in many ways it's a profound contradiction, but one that is essential for anyone focused on peace and reconciliation.

After ten days of visiting holy sites around Israel in 2003 and sitting with spiritual leaders from many traditions, most of the group had returned to their homes. Five others, including myself, stayed behind for three days to relax and visit several of our favorite spots without the constraints of a large group. One of those sites was the Dead Sea, particularly a resort and hot spring where the saline-rich water flows directly from the earth's core. The spring had been filled with tourists when we visited a few days earlier, but upon our return I was happy to find it nearly deserted. Of the five people in my group, only two of us decided to enter the pool, and it didn't take long before I was completely alone.

To back up a bit, a month earlier I had announced to my international email list that I would soon be offering a web-based class called "The Art of Spiritual Peacemaking." The fact that I had absolutely no idea what this class would include did not dissuade me from sending the announcement to over fifty thousand people. Weeks went by and excitement for the lessons began to build. Hundreds of people sent letters asking when the class would begin, a question I was still asking myself since I still had not received the inspiration required to write word one. I was beginning to wonder if I would ever receive clear direction, and worry was starting to build.

I believe I was thinking about this when I was soaking in the spring. Whether I was or not is of little consequence, though. I only know what happened next.

The water and the minerals seemed to inspire a deep contemplation, and I was unaware of anything other than the waves of deep relaxation washing through my whole being. Nothing else existed, and my spirit seemed to shake free from my body, my friends and the motionless sea. I was at peace, a vast and unfathomable peace, and I felt as if nothing would penetrate the stillness I felt.

Then I felt a presence, as if someone was standing next to me. I instantly realized, however, that it was not a body I felt beside me, but the spirit of a person I knew I recognized. In my mind I saw this spirit as a man who seemed to have walked straight out of the desert, his hair matted and his dark skin covered with sweat. But there was something else that caught my attention: his eyes. I had never seen eyes like this before, radiant and dazzling like the sun. He looked at me as if he saw more than the person floating there in the spring. He saw *me,* the me I rarely if ever saw myself. The love that shot from his eyes wrapped around me and filled me with Divine radiance. I knew, without his saying a word, that this was *he*: Jeshua, the real man who walked these same paths and roads two thousand years earlier.

I use the Aramaic name rather than the more common "Jesus" for a good reason. This was not the character from a book written nearly 2000 years ago, nor was it the man who had been painted by the great masters or whose image had been immortalized in statues on altars around the world. This was the real guy, the authentic man who walked and talked and ate with his friends two thousand years ago. The man I sensed next to me wasn't the cookie cutter Jesus but, rather, the mystical and passionate master who inspired or inflamed the land we now call holy. In an instant I knew why he inspired them so, for my own heart began to race.

All of this occurred without anyone around me even knowing. In other words, what I saw was within, not without, and yet it was more real than anything I had ever experienced before. Jeshua was there, and a conversation began that has shaped my life ever since.

"Would you like me to help you?" Those were the words I felt extending from him, and they startled me. What did he mean? What could he help me with? It was as if he knew what I was thinking. As he smiled I realized that he meant The Art of Spiritual Peacemaking course. "Would you like me to help you with it?" he asked again.

The way I was raised, you don't question such an extraordinary offer of support, especially when it comes from *him*. Still, I felt myself hesitate, as if I wasn't sure what it meant, or what I would be agreeing to. Luckily, the hesitation passed and I was convinced. "Yes, I do need you to help me."

Instantly, I felt something happen, as if information was being downloaded into my heart and my mind, information that I would have to access at a later date, regardless of how anxious I was to know what it was. He smiled when it was complete, then said to me, "When I was with my friends, I told them secrets that I couldn't reveal to the masses. They weren't ready...but now they are...you are and everyone else. Two thousand years ago I told them stories, but now is the time for everything to be revealed. That will be the course we will write together. I say together because it would be impossible for me to do it alone, just as it would be impossible for you to do alone. We need each other in this. And so, the lessons will be thirty-three in number, and each one of them will have exactly 999 words. Within them a code be present, one that will escape the intellectual mind, and it's this more than anything else that will teach them."

"What do you mean by code?" I asked.

"It's simple," Jeshua continued. "The information we will write together will have hidden information the conscious mind cannot comprehend. This information will be encoded within the words themselves. The soul will then hear what the mind cannot. In this way the secrets of the Kingdom will be revealed. They will be revealed in a way that each person may know and live them, for that is what is so needed today."

He smiled and I felt the vision begin to disappear, and whatever had been placed inside me seemed to glow and radiate. I immediately jumped out of the spring and ran to find my friends. I needed a pen and paper so I could write down everything I had just learned. When they saw me running toward them, they could see by the look in my eyes that I wasn't the same. They asked what had happened to me and I told them I couldn't talk then. I found what I needed and disappeared to a secluded table where I wrote everything I had heard from Jeshua.

Over 30,000 people signed up for the Art of Spiritual Peacemaking course, and I wasn't at all surprised by the response. I wasn't surprised because I shared their enthusiasm. I, as much as anyone, couldn't believe the power and insight of every lesson. Each day I would soak in hot water, just as I had done at the Dead Sea, and wait for something to happen. As I relaxed and felt myself expand, it was as if a door opened, and the next lesson would appear in my mind. I would then rush to the computer and type out what I felt, following the inspiration as long as it would last. And then, as suddenly as it had begun, it would end, and then I would look down at the word count on the computer: 80% of the time exactly nine hundred ninety-nine words. The other 20% was one or two words off, which I could easily adjust. Jeshua had been true to his word.

The second event that impacts the information in this book took place eight years earlier when I was traveling through war-torn Croatia and Bosnia. In the book *Emissary of Light* I described meeting a community of masters who claimed to have been fulfilling an ancient pact for the evolution of humanity.

Each night these thirteen men and women would enter a small meditation hut and would sit around a twelve-spoked wheel I later came to call "the Emissary Wheel." During the time I was with them I would sit in the domed hut as they conducted their rite, and I reveled at the power and energy that seemed to emanate from the geometric form drawn on the floor. Though I never understood the effects intellectually, something within me understood how important this wheel was. It was more than a symbol; it seemed to be a portal of some kind, with the power to transform and heal.

As the lessons with Jeshua proceeded, the Emissary Wheel became a focus of the instruction. Whether this was because I had already embraced it or it was a tool Jeshua himself used 2000 years ago is a mystery. I do, however, believe that he knew the sacred formula that is contained in the wheel. Jesus chose twelve apostles to stand around him and learn the mysteries he came to reveal. There was no coincidence here, for the entire technology of the Emissary Wheel is based on the "twelve around the one" energy, something that had been practiced in many esoteric fields of study. The Emissary Wheel, in all its forms, is one of the most magical and mysterious tools since the beginning of time. It is no wonder, then, that Jeshua places so much importance on its power throughout these lessons.

The third event was actually a realization that shaped my understanding and appreciation of this text. It would be easy to say that the material presented here was channeled: information from a master possessing the great wisdom and integrity it would require. There have even been times when it felt I was nothing more than a willing instrument to this power and that I was being used, albeit in a Divine manner, to bring this ancient wisdom to a modern era. And yet, as I said earlier, I believe that this explanation is too convenient and ultimately ineffectual. The purpose of this wisdom is to empower and reveal the inherent wisdom hidden within each one of us. So, beginning with a concept (and that is all it is —a concept) that there is another Master-Being outside of me, or outside any of us for that matter, communicating what we would not otherwise understand, would be the opposite of the real purpose and goal of this wisdom.

When I was in the hot spring at the Dead Sea, Jeshua asked me if I would be willing to write this "with" him. From the very beginning a pact seemed to exist making us equal partners, and though this was difficult to reconcile when I began to perceive the depth of this wisdom, it was nonetheless real. The information was not just coming "through" me, but also "from" me. If the basic premise of the lessons is true, that we are one with God and with each other, then the undeniable conclusion is that Jeshua and I are the same. We are one. In fact, it means that we are all the same, shining in the holiness in which we were created. It was not for me to "take" credit for this, but rather, to "accept" credit. In doing so I was accepting that Christ lives within me, and that there is nothing I can do to change that. This was the most empowering discovery of my life, and it is the real heart of this course.

Therefore, channeling in the traditional sense is impossible, since there is no one outside of me possessing any quality or innate wisdom that is not also mine. Perhaps this is the only message that has ever been received by such instruments or channels — namely, that we are still and will always be exactly as God created us. Once we realize that, as I did through this course, the rest happens on its own.

And so I present this as it was given. There is nothing here that you do not already know; perhaps it offers a window into what you already know. The secrets that Jeshua taught his friends 2000 years ago are not secrets at all, though we haven't been able to understand them till now. I know that this wisdom is real, and that it presents a key to remembering who we are and who we have always been. I pray that this key will unlock for you the very same door that I discovered within, and that once you enter you will realize that you never truly left your home.

James Twyman
November, 2005

Lesson One

Are you ready?

What other question need I ask of you? And what answer will you give now that it has been asked? Will you step forward, or back? There is no other choice. You have tried to hold still, but the days of waiting are now behind you. Are you ready to accept your mission, the one that was given to you before you were born? Are you ready to bring peace to all beings by BEING peace? Say YES! Say it loud enough that you may hear it. No one else need know. Only you. Only your soul.

You have been called to be a bearer of peace in this world of dreams. There is a reason for this. You want to wake up from this world, and it is the only way. Do you understand this? The only way for you to awaken is to awaken others. And yet, no one needs to wake up but you. Think about this for a moment. No one needs to awaken but you. Why, then, do I say that you must give this to receive it? It is so simple. Because you are only giving to yourself. There is no one there but you to give or receive.

Are you ready to see this, to know it, and to love it? If so, then you are ready to heal the whole world by being a Spiritual Peacemaker.

This whole course can be described in one sentence: "Give everything as if it is the only thing that matters, while knowing that God's will is perfect every moment." Meditate on this sentence for a moment. Give everything! It is already perfect! Nothing is required but your willingness to give everything to everything, and yet nothing you ever do will change the will of God that is fulfilled in every situation, no matter how it appears. Does this seem impossible to you? Why would you be asked to work for something if its outcome doesn't matter? That is what you are going to grapple with for the next 99 days, and when it is done you will understand, not with your mind, but with your soul.

Let me explain where I am leading you. There will be 33 lessons in this course that will flow through 99 days. Can you guess why this number is so important? Thirty-three is not an ordinary number. It is the number of your Christ consciousness. It is the number of your awakening. And why are these lessons being presented every three days? I laid motionless in the tomb for three days so that life would take me unto itself. I died that I might live forever, and you are being asked to do the same thing. The only way you can be a Spiritual Peacemaker is if you become the fulfillment of peace, or, in other words, if you become the Christ yourself. Do not be afraid of this, for I have gone before you to make straight the way. But make no mistake: now you must walk the path yourself. No one can do it for you. No one can accept life but you, and once done, it is accepted for all. This is the moment you chose, and it is fulfilled.

I am speaking to you on more levels than you know, for you exist on more planes of existence than you could ever realize with your mind. That is why these sacred numbers are so important, and these symbols I use will awaken this information in ways words never can. You will read the words and your mind will understand the concepts. Your life will benefit and you will touch the lives of countless others through the peace you offer. But there is so much more that the mind will never understand, and this is the critical place I am leading you now. These are the secrets that will transform your existence, just as they transformed me. Yes, I too underwent this transformation, and now I am a way-shower. You too will open the heart of this truth to those whom the Beloved gives you, just as you were given to me. There is no other reason you were born. Nothing else will mean anything to you, and yet you will not understand that until you offer it to everyone.

So now we will begin, for the journey has been laid out before us. Walk with me these 99 days, and let your mind be opened.

Two thousand years ago I shared mysteries with my friends that they held very sacred. They were only shared with others once they were prepared for the powerful impact of the truth upon their hearts and souls. Many of these secrets were encoded in a geometric symbol and was passed down from one community to another, and yet only a few of the people who were exposed to this symbol were able to unlock the secrets found within. Their souls knew and understood, but their minds were not yet ready to enter the sacred chamber.

But now it's critically important that all of you access this information. The secrets of the Kingdom of God are reflected there, for they are within you now. In the next 99 days I will open each lock and reveal for you the mysteries of life and death. Then you will understand the immortal nature of this quest, and you will know that you are one with the goal you seek.

So I'll ask you once again: Are you ready to enter upon this path? There will be moments when it will seem very dark, and others where the Light will almost blind you. Know that every step will be guided by me, for I have walked before you and I know every dangerous place. But you must know that your whole life has led to this moment. Then it will fall upon you like rain, refreshing your very soul.

—Brother

Lesson Two

Beloved. I call you by your name, for only then will you know the truth about your Self. Only then will you adopt the Holy Sight with which I see you and all beings. Then you will do as I do, extend that vision. The world is already healed, Beloved. That is what you have come to realize and learn. The world of dreams is now passing away, and you are left only with the Light of Peace. Welcome, Beloved, to your home.

It is important at this early stage for you to realize why you are here. First of all, why are you here on this Earth? Was it an accident of fate that brought you here, the aligning of circumstances beyond your decision? Or have you come far enough to realize that there is nothing beyond your decision? Nothing! Your birth at this time was predestined. It was pre- destined by you!

You are here because you chose it before time began. It was only an instant ago when you decided this, and now you are here. What will you do with this knowledge?

I will tell you. You will use time wisely to heal your split mind, then see the world as healed. Then it will be so, for you have the power of God within you. This is the moment when you are choosing to see your

Christ-Mind reflected everywhere, including where war seems to rage. Your decision alone will shed Light upon all these shadowy places, for the Light that proceeds from you is Holy Light. It is the Light that proceeds from my mind, and you are included there. You have come to KNOW this, and to heal through this knowledge. Blessed is the moment of this decision. And Blessed too is the world you will now heal.

Throughout the course of these 33 lessons I will offer suggestions to speed this process along. You are needed NOW. It is not because this time is any darker or more in need of your Light than any other time. It is simply because there is no other time but this. You are the one who chose this time. And you will fulfill everything you have set your heart upon. That is why it was important for you to open your heart before you could begin this stage. That is why you underwent the lessons that preceded this course, and now you are ready. You will bring it all with you, and you will see clearer than you have ever seen before. You are needed NOW, Beloved, and we will move forward with great speed.

It is not important that you understand or even accept the Mind that is sharing this information with you. It is your Mind as well. But the reference may be different, just as your view is different depending upon where you stand at a given moment. My reference is whole, while yours is still a bit splintered. That is about to change. It must change if you are to adopt the vision I would offer you. We will understand what we need to understand, and then we will set the intellect aside. It will not take us to where we need to go. But your heart, yes, this is where we will focus our attention. It is there already.

I want you to focus for a moment on the name I was given when I was born. Jeshua. If you can understand what this name means, and that it is yours as much as mine, then you will understand where we are headed together. You have been taught to chant the word YES to open the channels of your soul, preparing your heart for the Great Work that lies before us. It doesn't matter what language you use. It is the feeling you generate that creates the opening. There is a sound in Hebrew that essentially means "It is so." This is a more powerful interpretation of the word YES. The sound is *Yesh*. Say it a few times out loud. Make the sound long and draw it out for at least a few seconds. "Y-E-S-H." The sound generates a powerful response within your heart. See if you can sense the feeling. As one who has awakened his heart and mind to the experience of Christ consciousness, I can tell you that your dedication to this one word will lead you to where I am standing now. "It is so." Your Christ-Mind is *so*, this very moment. It is happening NOW, not in the future, not in the past. As you chant this sound over and over, let your heart awaken to this knowledge. "Y-E-S-H." It is *so* within you now. Your awakened mind is present, waiting for you to claim its power.

Now add the final sound "U-A." "Y-E-S-H-U-A." I am not the one you are chanting to. Do you realize this? I do not need this recognition, BUT YOU DO. My mind is your mind, and my name is yours. It is time for you to claim who you are. Chant it over and over, as often as you can. Call to the Christ in You, and it will awaken.

Will you believe me when I tell you that the rest will happen on its own? What do you wish to see in the world? Peace? Harmony? Adopt the vision that was given before time began and these things will appear before you. Why haven't they before now? Because you needed the world to reflect what you believed to be true. It is that simple. But now you are ready to allow a new Truth to dawn upon your mind, one that is eternal and beyond all change. It has always been there, but your eyes have been closed to its brilliance. Open now!

This is the essence of being a Spiritual Peacemaker. It is an art. It is your path to freedom. Choose peace now. You are ready.

—Brother

Lesson Three

Today I would speak to you about your passion and desire.

What do you hold dear in this world? Are you willing to offer everything you love to the One from whom all Love flows, knowing that only Love will return to you? Or do you believe that you must sacrifice what you love in order to have everything you desire? Be honest with yourself. What do you hold dear in this world?

Perhaps you will say your children, or your special relationship. What would happen to them if you completely accepted your role as an Emissary of Love, leaving behind all the things that do not serve that end? Would you still be able to provide for their needs? Would your relationship end, unable to compete with the great tide of energy that flows toward you even now?

Whether you are aware of it or not, these are some of the questions in your mind. You believe that a sacrifice is required of you, and that God would ask you to surrender all the things of time in order to embrace the eternal within. It is the natural state of the ego, which you still cling to. And yet, our goal is not to erase these conditions, for that would only amplify them. We desire only to focus on what is true, and to let that truth grow in our hearts and minds till all the symbols of fear are replaced.

You are afraid of love! Take a deep breath now. You will not be able to heal that wound until you embrace it. You will not be able to move to the next level of your Self unless you first accept your fear of love. Then your passion will be released on its own, without effort on your part. Then you will open like a flower, and your Holy Task will enfold you. Your fear of love will ultimately catapult you into a life you can only imagine now, for then you will have compassion for yourself and all the world. This is what an Emissary of Love, or a savior, must learn. That is why you are here now, reading these words and accepting these Blessed thoughts. You are ready to move forward now.

Your passion has been sleeping within you and must now be awakened. This will happen the moment you desire one thing. Your challenge has been that you desire more than one thing, and so you are not able to see that all desires are the same. If you choose in darkness, then shadows will enfold everything you perceive. But if you choose in the Light, then they will shine as you shine, and be blessed by your Holy Desire.

Passion and desire stand together in your mind and cannot be separated.

We will now open to the One Desire that will lead you to the goal you seek – the Peace of God. Nothing else in this world can satisfy you now. You have come too far. If I told you that you must desire only love, it would only confuse your mind. (Though this is, in fact, the final path we will walk together.) You have been given so many concepts of what love is and isn't, and they have only clouded your thoughts. Therefore, what we seek is the Peace that your mind can never comprehend, the Light that extends beyond all thoughts of time and space.

Your passion and desire are the keys that unlock this door. You must desire this over all things. All things! You must be willing to give up everything you perceive in this world in order to enjoy the Light that extends past this world. YOU MUST WANT IT ABOVE ALL THINGS. Only then will it be yours.

Pay attention for a moment to any emotions you are feeling right now. Did the thought of lack, in any degree, enter your mind? "What will I lose?" "Whom will I lose?" This is the basic dilemma of the ego: it has linked gain and loss, thinking that to accept everything you must sacrifice something else. Pay attention to this!

WHEN YOU ACCEPT EVERYTHING, NOTHING IS LOST! I once said that if you seek only the Kingdom of God, then everything else will be given to you automatically. When you seek only love, then love will return, and this is where your truest desire lies hidden. Love will flow to you from every direction, not just the ones you ordain. Life will find you; you won't have to find it. Therefore, let your passion be released and desire only the Gifts God would offer. Then your hunger will be satisfied, and your thirst will be forever quenched.

Then you will enter the Wheel of life. Then you will know yourself to be an Emissary of Love.

You are not here to bring worldly peace, but the Peace of God. You cannot understand this yet. Your mind will never be able to understand it. But the wider you open your heart the simpler it will become, until it is like a game children play. Then you will laugh where before you cried. Then you will know that love cannot be replaced by anything this world holds dear, for only love truly exists, now and forever.

Your desire is mine, and mine is yours. Are you willing to link your mind, and your passion, with mine? It is not the personality you are linking with, but the force behind the personality. This is what animates your

Spirit and mine, the Life that ignites all Life. This is the time you chose to undergo this transformation. Time can be your ally or a thief. Choose to use it wisely, and it will reveal the gifts that exist beyond your concept of time. There is nothing left for you to do now but embrace your passion for peace. Your desire is the path that will lead you to your chosen goal.

—Brother

Lesson Four

There was a time when you saw yourself as very distant from me. That time has now passed, for I have called you my friends, not my disciples. Now we can sit together by the fire, and I can tell you all the things that are so clear to me now. And then they will appear the same to you, not clouded and indistinct as they once were. Now is the time for us to relax and be as a family, for only then will you see that we are the same. My mind is yours, and the moment of my awakening was yours as well. Knowing this, I would like to share a story with you. Let the details sink into your mind, and the lesson into your heart, that you may understand where this path is leading us.

Imagine a house that is filled with Light. There is nothing in this house save a small, unimaginably brilliant crystal in the very center that reflects and magnifies the Light that streams in from every window. The room needs nothing, though there is nothing there. The Light vibrates with an essence that in unseen, indescribable, and you are content to exist there in Perfect Joy.

Then one day a new thought arises. It will not do to have such an empty house. It is so calm and comfortable there that there should be a place for "You" to sit. Many chairs are brought in and couches that fill every room. Then the thought arises that there must be a place for "You" to dine, for eating in the comfortable chairs will not do. And so you buy tables and place them in the appropriate places, and more chairs to place around the tables. Then you look around and see that there is no bed for "You" to sleep in. And so you go out and purchase a bed for yourself that is soft and luxurious, and others beds in case you have guests. Day after day you fill the house with all the furnishings you desire, until the moment comes when you see that there is enough.

But something else has changed as well. You look around the house and realize that the Light that once radiated from every corner has been dimmed. You find lamps to add more light, but no matter how many lamps you buy it never equals the brilliance you once knew. You go and sit in your favorite chair, the one in the very center of the house. As you sit, you remember the crystal. It was almost forgotten in the rush of filling the house with everything "You" needed to be comfortable. You look at the crystal and you can see a faint glow you once knew, the Light that once filled your days. Then a new thought enters your mind. You look around for the "You" that was so important, the one you bought so much furniture and decorations for. Where is this elusive being that required so much? No matter how hard you look you cannot find the "You" that was so important a short time ago. Maybe there is too much furniture to find "You." One by one the chairs are removed, then the couches, and even the tables. You go upstairs and remove the beds, and the lamps, and everything else that you bought. Finally, you look around and notice something amazing.

You are ready! The Light has returned!

And you are standing right where you started. All the furniture that blocked the Light from the crystal is gone, and the whole house vibrates with Life. And you vibrate as well, for you know that you are that crystal, and that Light, and that house, and that "You."

The time we are spending together, all these lessons, are meant to help the Light return to your mind. We will not accomplish this task by adding anything, but by subtracting all the things that have blocked the Light from your conscious experience. The crystal, or your awakened soul, will be enough. Nothing else is required.

Where is the "You" you are seeking? Does it exist at all, or was it simply a concept used to distract your pure awareness? Who is it that is seeking? Your thoughts have created this being, and your thoughts can uncreate it as well, revealing the Truth that you can neither create nor uncreate. This is what we are seeking today.

Simply put, the "You" that is being sought does not exist. Rejoice in this, for the realization of this fact is the beginning and the end of your journey.

Who are you, then? You are the crystal that reflects the Light. The Light is full within this crystal, fully contained and fully realized. You cannot change, and whatever there is in you that seems to change is not who you are. Play with it if you choose, but do not cling to it. Cling only to the eternal essence beyond your influence, and then you will see that there is nothing beyond your influence. Do you understand the subtle difference here?

The Art of Spiritual Peacemaking is the art of removing the blocks to your Light. Then the Light shines on its own. You do not need to "do" anything. You just need to "BE" who you already are. You are the Light of Eternal Grace. You are the Pure Essence of the Being of God. Stop trying to understand this with your mind. It is the surest way to never KNOW it. Simply understand that it is true NOW, this very instant, fully revealed, WHETHER YOU ARE AWARE OF IT OR NOT!

The Art of Spiritual Peacemaking has nothing to do with changing anyone, including yourself. It is the deep comprehension that there is no one to change, including yourself. Then your eternal Self is revealed, and everything falls into its natural place. If you decide to enter this portal now, you can.

—Brother

Lesson Five

I have called you to remember the reason you chose to be born. You have chosen to answer that call, for the song that was planted in your soul is now ringing in your ears. This is the time YOU chose to awaken and BE. The time of dreams has now passed, for your help is required to initiate a world that has never been threatened, except in your imagination. You will now release those imaginings for the world Peace will show. This is the only thing you desire now, and thus is your release assured.

I will not call you to BECOME anything, but to BE all things. How can I ask you to COME to me when I do not see any distance between us at all? I ask you to BE me. Are you beginning to understand? There is nowhere for you to go. You need only open your eyes and see where you have always been. Will you answer this call and assume your rightful place at my side? Does it help to say that I need you here, for the All is not known in my mind unless it's known in ALL? Stand now and be seen with the family you have chosen to awaken, and be awakened by. Know that the time is NOW. There is no other path for you to walk now but the path of Peace. All is answered there.

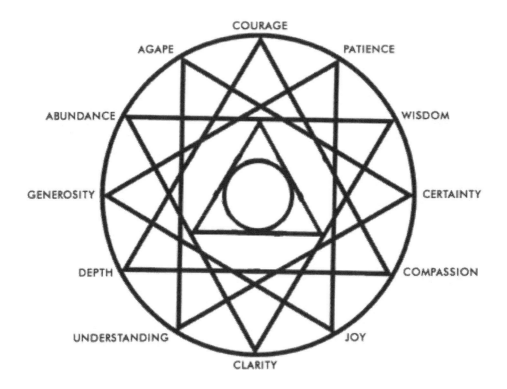

I will begin speaking to you now about the wheel of wisdom and life. You have called this the Emissary Wheel because it was the sacred focus of many ancient communities and groups for thousands of years. It contains information, profound information, and we will now begin using this information consciously that we may comprehend the proper way to accept our role of being Spiritual Peacemakers in this world. These ancient groups have closely guarded this information, but there is no more time to waste. The wheel itself will speak to your heart and mind, but only if you possess the foundation that will allow this knowledge to take root in your soul.

Look at the wheel for a few moments and let it speak to you. Don't worry about focusing at one particular point. Let your eyes move where they will and trust that they are being guided by the energy emanating from this sacred geometry. The mysteries of peace and life itself are encoded here, and you have the key that will unlock the door that leads to all the answers you desire. Let your soul absorb this code, knowing that it will be revealed when the time is right. You may feel powerful pulsations moving through you as you look. Do not resist any of it, but allow yourself to flow into and through this portal. It will be your teacher, and you will grasp its secrets. That is all you need to know for now, only that the ending is sure. That should be enough to inspire your continued movement toward the Center that does not move.

Now, pay attention to the twelve points that touch the outer circle of the wheel. This is where we will begin our lessons, for it is here that you will touch where you are and who you are this and every moment. Each of these twelve points represents a quality of energy associated with a Spiritual Peacemaker. These

are the qualities you must amplify during the next
several months as you progress through this training.
You may want to have a separate copy of the wheel
where you will write these qualities at each point.
Always begin at the twelve o'clock point and move
clockwise around the wheel. Here are the twelve
qualities:

- **Courage**

- **Patience**

- **Wisdom**

- **Certainty**

- **Compassion**

- **Joy**

- **Clarity**

- **Understanding**

- **Depth**

- **Generosity**

- **Abundance**

- **Agape**

Over the next four lessons we will discuss these
qualities in groups of three, since the qualities

themselves are grouped energetically. In three days we will begin with Courage, Patience and Wisdom. I will ask you to join me in experiments that will enlighten these qualities and help them dissolve into your soul. Once you have integrated each of the twelve, then we will begin moving in through the spokes and explore the deeper lessons the wheel can teach us. For now it is enough to know that all your questions will be answered here, not with words, but with the Light that transcends all words. It is this Light we are seeking together.

Over the next three days meditate with the Emissary Wheel as much as you can. You may feel powerful releases taking place in you as you conduct this practice. If this happens, simply breathe deeply and let them flow in whichever direction needed. Even if your experience is profound and rapturous, know that the energy itself is clearing a path for you to walk toward your Self. All is well. There is nothing that can happen to you here. You need only surrender to the current of grace that is flowing through this symbol and realize that the current is your very life.

Which brings me to the final and most important thing I can tell you at this time. This wheel, this symbol, is who you are. It is nothing more, and nothing less, than a geometric representation of your Highest Self. It is Perfect Balance which you can know and enjoy this moment. Do not think that these mysteries will lead anywhere but back to where you are now and always. There is nowhere else for you to go. The wheel is meant to awaken the part of you that is still sleeping, the larger part of you that has hidden from your Divinity. There is no reason to hide now. You have come too far to turn back. There is only one direction: Forward. Focus now on the wheel, and in doing so, on your Self. This is the moment you have been waiting for.

—Brother

Lesson Six

Today we enter a sacred wheel that is the symbol of your enlightened mind. Know that you are being called to see yourself as you are, and as you have always been. Let me try to express that thought more clearly. You are here for one reason and one reason only: to know that you are enlightened NOW. No other goal will do. You can step into this experience right now if you choose. Do you? Let me tell you the first thing you must do if you are to accept and embrace this Holy Mind:

> *Let go of every thought you have ever had*
> *about what it means to be enlightened.*

I mean this literally. Do not hold onto a single concept of what you think it means to walk the earth as an enlightened being. Why? There is only one thing I can guarantee at this point—that every thought you have about this is wrong. How do I know this? Because the goal we seek has nothing to do with the concepts and thoughts you hold. They are all blocks to your Holy Awareness, no matter how sacred they seem. If you want to KNOW who you are, then KNOW who you are. No thought can take you there, only your

27

recognition of what has always been true and can never change.

Today we will enter the sacred wheel that has been a symbol of this awakening for thousands of years. You will be asked to embrace each of the twelve qualities of an Emissary of Light, which are the portals into the experience we are seeking. As you read this information, look at the wheel itself.

Let your eyes wander through the geometric patterns that are meant to awaken your soul at a super-conscious level. You do not need to understand it intellectually. In fact, you cannot understand it intellectually. Strive to embody the qualities I will offer your mind, and let your soul seek its own path through the spokes of the wheel. These are the qualities we will explore for the next three days. If possible, read one of these sections each day, or refer back to them every day. Breathe them into your life, and they will exhale you into a New Life.

Courage:

It is not the courage of this world we are seeking, but of the Real World from which you came and where you have always belonged. You have forgotten this Sacred Home, and yet you have never really left.

Courage is the first path that will lead to your Remembering. Everything in the world of form forces you into a place of weakness. Separation itself is weakness, and so you must deny its effect before you can adopt true courage. You aren't alone. The "you" that you think you are doesn't exist in truth. Only the "You" God perceives exists, and this is where we will gain our courage. It cannot be threatened. Such a thing is impossible. Death cannot touch the "You" God perceives, so there is nothing to be afraid of in this world. To the ego, death is victory, for it proves its version of the world true. But the death the ego perceives is an illusion. It is not a real end. Why, then, would you choose to be afraid of this impossible conclusion? Be courageous and know that you are an eternal being. The body's decay is not yours, for you are not your body. Are you afraid of the clothes you wear falling to ruin on some future date? Why would you be afraid of the body's natural end? Release this fear and everything else will fall into its natural place, and you will be afraid of nothing. To be an Emissary of Light means that you focus on what is, not what isn't, and you find your courage there. Let go of the concept of death, and you will discover a wealth of strength you didn't know you possessed. Today I ask that you imagine yourself to be the enlightened being I perceive, filled with courage. Imagine how you would walk through this world if this courage were yours. Your meditation will be to spend some time imagining this new life today.

Patience:

There is no time in which you will be judged. There is only NOW, and you have already accepted the finality of your soul's TRUTH. Understand this and Divine Patience will be yours. Then time will have no meaning to you, for you will know the ultimate conclusion of your life: Full knowledge of your True Self. How can you be anything but patient if you know the path you walk? Even if you do not see the castle in the distance, still you are certain of your eventual arrival. And the more certain you are of this, the sooner you will perceive this reality. Only Divine Patience offers immediate results. There is no hurry, then, for the ending is sure. Enjoy the path you walk and admire the beauty of the landscape. Turn one more corner and you are there. Today I ask that you imagine yourself to be the enlightened being I perceive, filled with patience. Imagine how you would act toward others if this patience were yours. Imagine this new life, and embrace it now.

Wisdom:

Is it the wisdom of the world you seek, or of God? Which will you choose, for I tell you, they are not the same. The wisdom of the world tells you to understand the multitude of differences that lie before you, while the wisdom of God tells you there is no difference. There is no real difference between you and anyone else, and there is no time in which the holiness you share is compromised. How can this lead to anything but Perfect Joy? Imagine that you are an enlightened being, filled with wisdom. You are. I see it so clearly. Can you?

— Brother

Lesson Seven

We have embarked on a Sacred Journey together. It is a journey without distance that leads to where YOU have always been. The mind has been laid aside, as has the body that you made with your mind. Your thoughts have brought you to this place, but they cannot lead you to where you really belong. We travel from here together, wrapped within one another, one heart and one mind ascending to the Higher Kingdoms. You have tried to come alone, but have seen that such a journey was impossible. Everything you created comes with you now to the Home you never left.

You may wonder about the value of the geometric form we have chosen to employ on this journey, the Emissary Wheel. It is true that no symbol can cross this barrier, and yet it can aid you in your journey to the gate of that Holy Experience. Ultimately the only symbol you are being asked to lay aside is your own "self concept." You have forgotten who you are and have adopted an image you cling to till your body's death, and you continue on with a new image that seems to change. And yet, who you really are does not change, for it exists beyond the world of transient reality. This is what you are here to discover, and the symbol of the Wheel will serve as a tool to initiate that awakening. Then we will lay it aside, just as we will lay all symbols aside, and rest together in the Kingdom beyond your dreams.

The twelve spokes of the Emissary Wheel represent the twelve aspects of your ego's dream. Their points exist on the outer fringe of the wheel, and therefore seem most separate. But now we have given them new meaning, and have adopted the tools of transformation that lead to the inner dimensions of your Life. These are the experiences we are looking at now, and as we continue walking this path we find ourselves moving closer to the center of the wheel. Then we exist in the place that does not move, the place where your dreams of separation have no meaning. That is the goal of this course, and it is how you will know yourself to be a Spiritual Peacemaker and an Emissary of Light.

Today we will open our hearts to the next three spokes and the experiences they inspire. You will find that they are grouped together in threes, resulting in four triangles, or twelve spokes. Each experience leads to the next and is meant to deepen your comprehension of the Truth within. We will deal with the concepts for now since we cannot describe Reality itself. Open your heart to them and gaze at the wheel, and the lessons I cannot describe with words will be revealed on their own.

The fourth spoke:

Certainty:

You are not asked to believe anything, but to KNOW. In the past I spoke of the importance of your belief, but that was when you were a child. Now you are mature, and so I treat you in a new way. Lay your belief aside, and KNOW that you are One with me and all Reality. Your belief has led you to the door of Awakening, but only your Certainty will allow you to enter. Otherwise you will stand there and never comprehend. I will lead you forward, for I am Certain of who you are. But it is time for you to be Certain as well. Only then will you be able to See the Beauty that I perceive within you. You will not be able to See it anywhere until you KNOW it is yours. Your Certainty is required now.

The fifth spoke:

Compassion:

Perfect Certainty leads to Perfect Compassion. When you are Certain of who you are then you will Know that it extends beyond the shallow definitions you once held of yourself and the world. How can you experience Compassion for what lies beyond you? But what lies within, yes, this you can have Perfect Compassion for, and everything lies within. I will say that again so there is no possibility of confusion: Everything lies within. When you know who you are then your Wisdom is Perfect, and your Compassion is perfect as well, for you will realize that every gift you give is given to yourself. Open your heart in Love, and know that love returns to you. Where else would it lead but to the source you never left?

The sixth spoke:

Joy:

Perfect Compassion leads to Perfect Joy. Are you beginning to see how each one of these Holy Experiences leads to the same place and cannot exist without the others? Your Joy has never been complete because your awareness was splintered. You have chosen to look upon what is not real and deny what is. There have been moments when you have laughed and moments when you have felt the sudden movement of your heart. But the joy we seek now does not depend upon the movements of this world but of the Real World that cannot change. Then you will live where you choose to live, and do what you choose to do, and yet never leave the Sacred Ground of your Perfect Joy. Your heart will be fixed on what is Real within you, not that which has never existed. Simply put, you will finally be able to understand the difference. Do you understand how valuable this will be? You will walk upon the Earth as I walked, untouched by the changing tides of unreality, blessing everything you touch because you see the truth that exists within YOU. You will be a Savior, and the example of your life will be enough to enlighten any darkened mind that comes to you.

You have been called to save the world by Seeing as God Sees and Knowing What God Knows. Will you accept this commission? Will you finally choose Peace?

—Brother

Lesson Eight

You have chosen to be an instrument of peace, or a Spiritual Peacemaker. I have not chosen you, you have chosen yourself. I want you to understand this subtle but important difference. I cannot ask you to do anything that you have not already chosen. Even if I could I would not try, for it would place you below me, and such a position is not appropriate. We stand together, and so I have called you my friends. The work we have chosen must be completed by us all, since it is "for" us all. Are you beginning to understand how important your role is?

I would like to speak to you now about the attributes you are learning to embody that will allow you to step fully into your role of being a Spiritual Peacemaker.

You now realize how each of these attributes, all of which an Emissary of Light must fully contain, all of which you do fully contain this moment, deepen as they progress. Each one prepares the way for the next, until the each spoke of the whole wheel has been gathered together as one radiant form, representing the radiant YOU that is emerging from the place you have hidden.

As I said, you contain each of these this very moment, whether you are conscious of it or not. It does not matter if you are conscious of it at this point, and the moment you realize that your conscious recognition of this does not matter will be the same moment they break through. All that is important at this stage is that you recognize each of these traits as yours NOW — not becoming, not gradually integrating, but fully present this very moment. Then you will be given a marvelous gift from the Spirit of Truth that waits for you now. You will be able to see it everywhere else, and then you will stand at my side as a miracle worker, a Spiritual Peacemaker, and an Emissary of Light.

Do you think that it matters to me what you think of yourself? It doesn't. Do you think that it has ever occurred to me to enter into your self-concept and validate it in any way? It hasn't. My joy is to see you as you really are, not as you imagine yourself to be. It does not occur to me to ask you if you see it as well, for such a thought would give reality to what isn't real. I gaze upon the Light in you, regardless of what you perceive. You are now ready to see that this is what you are being asked to do, as well, for it is the highest calling. And this is the time you have chosen to do this, for your brothers and sisters need you now. Look upon them with gentle eyes and do not acknowledge the visions of separation they perceive. Acknowledge only the Truth, the Grace that flows through them this moment and the next. That is how you will ground the same vision of yourself, for you cannot give this gift without receiving it.

The seventh spoke:

Clarity:

You have been looking at the world with unfocused eyes and have made all your decisions based upon subtle misunderstandings of the Universe you thought you saw. And yet you have not realized your misperception and believe that you see clearly. Now a friend, a Brother, comes to you and gently points at the things you thought you saw, and helps you understand that they are not the demons and monsters you thought they were. It is like putting glasses on for the first time. My Clarity becomes yours, and you are finally able to See. How will you do this? First of all, by accepting that you have not seen clearly until now. Without Guilt. Then you will trust that I understand what you have confused. Finally, your gratitude for your meaningless error will bring the Clarity you have lacked till now, and everything will make sense again.

The eighth spoke::

Understanding:

Until now your goal has been to be understood by others, and so you have lacked the understanding that you really desire. You cannot understand something until you See it clearly, comprehending what it really is. And you cannot know who you are until you are willing to offer that same gift to another. Try to understand the Holiness of whoever is standing in front of you now, not with your mind, for you will surely fail. Try to feel the Grace, and then KNOW that it is yours. I ask only that you understand who you are. You will not be able to accept your role of power until then. You will know this by giving it, for understanding is a gift that is given and received at the same moment. Do you long to See who you are, then understand that it is the same SELF God perceives? Then SEE as God SEES, and Understand what is real. Your Seeing is the key to everything.

The ninth Spoke:

Depth:

It is not the depth of this world we are seeking together, but of the world beyond your imagination. And yet, when you finally begin to perceive this Real World as it truly is, then it impacts the world you created with your mind. In truth they are the same, though one is only a splinter of the beauty you could know, if only you would open your heart. It is the choice you must make, and this is the moment you will decide. It may be better to say that it is the moment you "did" decide, since the choice was already made. This is the thought that inspires your depth, the understanding that your decision has already been made, and so has the result of that decision. And what is the result? Simply this – perfect acknowledgment of who you are. What else is there to seek?

—Brother

Lesson Nine

Today we will begin with a thought that is the foundation of your work as a Spiritual Warrior. It is the experience you seek and the reward you will enjoy. When it is full within you, when you can say this phrase with complete confidence, then you will know that you have arrived at the place where your gifts can be offered to the Spirit of Truth. The Spirit will then use you, as you, and you will KNOW why you arrived on this planet.

"My cup runs over."

Say this phrase over and over and try to feel the energy that enfolds your soul. What does this mean to you, and how can you become the cup that flows with Divine Grace? Isn't this what you are really seeking? How can you give something to another unless you have fully realized it yourself? Do not think that in your humanness you are able to purge the urge toward self-promotion: it may not reflect the Truth in you, but the ego has always been a welcomed guest in your home. You soon forget that it was invited to remain, though you did not have to extend its stay. You cannot purge it, but through Grace it can be removed from you. This will occur only if you fully accept it and offer it the opening it desires: Integration rather than extinction. Then it leaves on its own, and you are able to See who you really are, the Self you have remained even while you dreamed of impossible worlds.

"My cup runs over."

Be filled with the Peace you desire to share. Don't ask for anything, for it is the admission that it is not already yours. How can you desire something that you do not know, and ultimately, do not have. What is needed is an expansion of what it means to possess something. Your role is simply to realize that there is nothing in this universe that is not full within you. There is nothing you can conceive that is not already yours. This realization, then the experience, is what it means to "Spill God's Grace Everywhere." You are a living vessel, a holy tabernacle, and yet, God cannot use you until you step toward your Self, the "You" that cannot be threatened by your illusions. Until now you have stepped away into the dream you created, and so you have understood what it means to be weak and alone. But every dream must end, and so do you now step away toward the reality we share. KNOW this, then give it to all. Only then will your cup continue to overflow. Only then will you enjoy the riches that have always been yours.

"My cup runs over."

This will be your prayer for the next few days. Meditate with it, but most of all "feel" the prayer in your heart. It is true, but you will directly experience this truth only as you extend it to others. This brings us to the final three spokes of our Emissary Wheel.

Tenth Spoke:

Generosity:

Why would you hold back when you realize you are only denying yourself? This is the single barrier that needs to be removed, for there is still a place in you that believes that if you give something to another, then you have lost it yourself. Loss can only occur in your mind, but is then translated into your physical life. Were you to remove the concept altogether then you would not think to look at the outward appearance of things to determine anything. You would feel abundance because you would offer it to everyone. Your cup would run over and would be continually refilled. The universe itself is conspiring to bring you this, but you have resisted it and have therefore created an experience that seems to set you at odds with reality. Stop trying to determine what is yours and what belongs to another.

There is no other! There is only You waking from the dream of separation. You have been called to be a Spiritual Peacemaker, and the world cannot possibly understand what this means. That is because everything in the world you created reflects the laws of a world that does not exist except in your imagination. Give everything to everything! If you hold back your gift then you are the one who will suffer, and suffering is no longer necessary.

Eleventh Spoke:

Abundance:

Do you want the world of form to reflect your inner KNOWING? You already realize that each spoke in this wheel leads to the next, and so your generosity automatically leads to your abundance. It is almost redundant to speak of this for if you have been following the direction of this Divine Thought then you would know this already. You are here to have everything you desire. There is no sacrifice for you to make, though I guarantee that your priorities will change when you accept this new role. You may begin to define abundance in new ways when you don't expect the outside world to reflect your inner reality.

There are those among you who have next to nothing by the standards of the world, and yet they are the most abundant. There are also those who have everything, and yet they are the poorest among you. Make your choice about what you desire to fully receive. Once again, GIVE EVERYTHING TO EVERYTHING and you will remember who you are and why you are here.

Twelfth Spoke:

Agape:

You are here to adopt the vision of God that automatically leads to the Love of God. We call this Agape, for it indicates an experience wholly unlike your concepts of love. God's love depends on nothing, and so it is unconditional. You have been called to Love as God Loves. Quite simply, it is the only thing that can give you everything you desire. Are you ready to lay everything else on the altar now?

—Brother

Lesson Ten

The Three Enlightenments

Now that we have finished examining the twelve qualities of the Spiritual Peacemaker we are ready to consider the real function of the Emissary Wheel. To some it is a simple geometric symbol that communicates information on psychic and spiritual levels. I have also said that it is an outer symbol of an inner journey, or in other words, the journey of your personal transformation. Now we will open our minds and hearts to its true function, that of being an energy portal able to shift the intention of your human experience into a Divine context. When you realize and experience this Divine Context, then you will be able to fulfill your role on this planet.

You may have already noticed certain powerful or subtle shifts that occur within even when gazing at the Emissary Wheel. We will discuss this at great length as we progress through this course, but it is important for you to realize that what you are feeling is very real. Certain geometric shapes have the ability to produce physical and spiritual reactions just by focusing on them. Most of you have already realized this and have had your own experiences that help you understand. The particular form that we have employed has been used for thousands of years by the ancient mystery schools in Egypt, then later adopted by certain esoteric Christian traditions, most particularly the "Community of the Beloved Disciples" founded by the man you refer to as St. John, and whom I call my friend. He was able to crystallize the truths and teachings I offered, then activate them through the wheel. It has since been used by the extensions of that original community to project a powerful energy, or focused communal prayer, that has kept humanity moving forward on its spiritual evolutionary track. The Emissaries of Light were the most recent group to conduct this powerful meditation and use the wheel, but they were far from the first. Now it falls to you, for the fact that you are reading this now means that you have been called. The form you choose to extend this is up to you. It does not matter at all. But the transformation the wheel will cause is important indeed, and that is why much of this course will be focused on it.

For the next three weeks we will focus our attention on the fruit of this transformation, what we will call the "Three Enlightenments." They are: Illumined Mind, Awakened Heart, and Realized Soul.

The twelve qualities we have examined for the last several lessons make up the first Enlightenment, the second is found in the inner triangle, and the circle in the middle of the wheel represents the third. Ultimately, here is what you have come to learn through all of this: The quality of God's Love is the same as the quality of your Love of God. That is what we are here to achieve, this recognition. Your first inclination will be to try to understand this statement intellectually. Hopefully you will realize the impossibility of this rather quickly. The mind cannot understand what it has no relationship to. And yet there is an experience that exists beyond the mind that can translate these concepts into tangible truths. The mind will be empty and serene, yet will you understand. It has been set aside for a moment in favor of a deeper ocean, one that will withstand the crashing waves of thought. Once you have touched this place, nothing else will suffice. Then the Peace of God, that which surpasses all thought, will be yours, and you will stand at my side to save the world.

Today we begin by considering the quality of God's love, that which you must understand even at the most basic level, then compare it to your love of God. There is a mystery here, and if you are able to see the correlation between these two, then experience it in your heart, your progress will be swift. We will begin in the mind but, as always, seek the deeper pulse from which all real learning occurs. One of these extends from God while the other returns. The mind believes that these are two actions; you have already come far enough to realize that it is really one. What extends from God stays with God. What extends from you stays with you. If there really are two of you in this equation, you and God, then it would mean that no movement has occurred at all. God has not moved toward you and you have not moved toward God. Therefore, one of two things is false, either the premise itself, or the concept of "two." You can decide for yourself.

What extends from God is perfectly received by God. God gives but to Itself, and you are not separate from that giving. YOU ARE THAT GIVING. It is who you are, yet you have tried to deny who you are. Thankfully, you have failed miserably at this attempt, and nothing has changed at all. You seem to have changed since the perceived Split, but there is a rather large difference between something "seeming" to happen, and actually happening. Your failure is your salvation. It should be embraced, not decried. Then you can look at yourself again and see that you are the Gift of God and the Giving of God at the same moment. Another more simple way of saying this, which you already know, is that you are One with God. Now we come full circle, back to the place we began. I could have said this at the beginning and you would have understood, but this winding path has a purpose, though you are not able to perceive it quite yet. That moment, however, is fast approaching.

So what is the experience that exists beyond the mind that can translate this into tangible truths? Your Unconditional Surrender! Embrace it now.

—Brother

Lesson Eleven

We are on a journey of awakening. In reality this is a journey that leads back to where you have always been. No distance has been crossed, for you have never truly left your Home. The Thought of God has never left its source, and that thought has been identified as You. And now a new Light dawns upon your open mind, for you have begun to embrace an ancient experience that leads to your full Illumination. Your enlightenment is at hand, and the Grace of your birthright suddenly fills your soul.

The awareness of your enlightenment will occur in three stages. This is what we are calling the "Three Enlightenments."

Illumined Mind, Awakened Heart, Realized Soul

Notice that I referred to this as the "awareness of your enlightenment." This is the critical distinction that must be observed then accepted before any real shift occurs. YOU ARE ALREADY ENLIGHTENED! In fact, there is nothing but this seemingly elusive state in the whole Universe, perfectly revealed every moment as You. You cannot choose whether this is true or false, but you can choose whether you are conscious of it.

Until now you have chosen to live within the ego's tight constraints, completely misidentified by its version of who you are and what the world is for. But now a Light has opened in your mind, and you are at least able to consider the possibility that you are so loved of God that Grace wrapped itself around you the instant you were conceived by Eternity, and enfolds you still. As you surrender to this Love you will feel yourself waking up to the vision of the Real World, a place where time does not exist and your Holiness shines forever. First your mind will open, then your heart, and finally your whole soul. Over the next several lessons we will examine these stages and how you can use the Emissary Wheel to excite the process.

The First Enlightenment:

Illumined Mind

This is the Light that shatters your perception of everything you thought was real and everything you value in the world. Its effect is stronger than anything you can consider with you mind. Imagine that you have been sitting in a dark closet for many years when suddenly the door opens to a cloudless sky. The sun is directly above and you are blinded by its effect. Now multiply this by one hundred, then one thousand, and you are then close to the powerful opening you will experience when the First Enlightenment dawns. You will see the world through new eyes and believe that you have finally arrived at the end of your journey. But you have not. It is but the first stage of your awakening, and it is essential that you do not accept this. The contrast alone is enough to convince you that you must have achieved full illumination, but the ego still clings to the walls of your mind and is afraid to move forward. (We will define the ego as the part of YOU hat believes it is separate from everything that exists. It is not real, just as YOU, or the concept of YOU, is not real. This is your salvation.) You now look out upon the world you created and realize that you created it. Do you understand? You are no longer the effect, but the cause, and thus do you realize your power. But power without an awakened heart is nothing, and so we move on to the second stage.

The Second Enlightenment:

Awakened Heart

You will recognize a master who has achieved the second stage by their willingness to give everything to everything. How can you hold back when the whole universe is giving to you every moment? Your heart explodes and becomes a river of refreshment to all beings. They come to you with parched tongues and drink from the Grace that flows from deep within. When you look upon them you see only the Beloved, for you know that only the Beloved exists, and your praise is unmatched. Words cannot speak of this state, for they are but the concepts of a world that no longer exists for you. And yet there is a new language you have learned, the language of the heart, of Love itself. You are that Love NOW. The instant the Second Enlightenment occurs the first thing you will say to your Self is "How could I have not seen this before? It is the most obvious thing in the Universe." And so it is with you and all beings, for the Awakened Heart reveals that which cannot change within you. But you are still not finished. There is still one final opening, the third stage.

The Third Enlightenment:

Realized Soul

Of this we cannot speak. The moment you try to conceptualize this state is the instant you return to the world of form, the world the Realized Soul views but through half-opened eyes. It would not be true to say that they are in the world at all, just as you are not in the world even now. But the true master sees both within them, and thus becomes the bridge that leads others into the vast Light of Realization. Stand beside them and you are but a step away. Enter yourself and you realize that there is no step at all. It was all in your mind, then your heart, and it is now but a memory that fades as does the darkened sky come dawn. The shadows that frightened you so appear as harmless friends, and you find yourself wrapped in a deep incomprehensible peace. You are home, the home you never left except in your imagination. There is nowhere for you to go now, for the Light has come to you at last.

And yet, through these three stages of your enlightenment, nothing has changed at all. You are the same as you have ever been.

— Brother

Lesson Twelve

I have called you my Beloved Friends, my family, because I have looked upon your Love and recognized you as my own. Now you must do the same, for to fully enjoy this Sacred Union we must see with the same eyes, perceive the world through the same heart, and know the Beloved every moment we live. The Three Enlightenments are not real, for they do not indicate any real change in you. But they seem real because your heart has been closed for so long, and it is finally returning to its most natural state. That is the only thing that is important right now.

I have said that you are already enlightened, and that is why I know myself, because I have seen this in you. How else would I understand the ways of my Father/Mother if not by giving what I have received? Are you willing to step into this same Light now? You have come here only for this, and this is the moment you decided to awaken long before you were born into this body. Look upon the world with new eyes now, and you will understand everything I have said, not with your mind, but your whole Self.

Look upon the Emissary Wheel for a moment and notice the outer circle where all the points meet. Let your gaze soften and you will notice that the Wheel seems to move on its own. Your focus will shift from one place to another, and you will see triangles upon triangles, all leading to the very center where no movement occurs at all. This is your goal, perfect stillness. We begin on the outer reach where the circle encloses the wheel, then begin to move inward through the spokes until we arrive at the center triangle. You are now a step away from Heaven, for there is nothing left but to release everything you thought was real. Then all your questions fade and melt before this altar of Grace, and you at last perceive your Blessed Holiness. Scales fall from your eyes and you see the world as if for the first time. Nothing can invade this calm, for you have broken free from the restraints of what never happened at all. This is the only moment that exists, for you remember who you are, and all is well.

I have called you to stand at my side as Spiritual Peacemakers. This is what is meant by the phrase: "Be in the world but not of the world." You must become the bridge that leads others into the Light we share, away from the world you thought was real, into the World where reality is never threatened. A simple loving glance in the direction of another can bring more peace than all the governments in the world. A hand extended to another frees more energy than all the sources of power on this planet. We lay aside our former judgments and view the world through spiritual eyes. We are not interested in results, but in the peace that surpasses all understanding. The Emissary Wheel is valuable only because it is patterned after your Awakened Self. On its own it has no value at all, but when applied to this holy moment it releases you from the prison you placed yourself within.

Is this what you choose now? You must have realized that you are in prison; otherwise you would have never answered the call I sent forth. And how do you feel when I tell you that the door to your cell was never locked? You could have left at any moment, and yet your fear of what lay outside kept you from experiencing the freedom you deserve. Reach out and turn the handle and you will see for yourself. It turns easily, almost too easily. You may feel the temptation to criticize yourself for not having left before. But how could you be of service to others if you never experienced all these things? I too felt this prison, and now I look back upon you and call you forward into the Light I enjoy. As soon as you leave you will do the same, then you will know what a peacemaker really is. Until now you have imagined that a peacemaker is one who brings peace to the world. All I am here to show you is that there is no world to bring peace to. Don't try to understand these words with your mind for you will surely fail. You have come far enough to comprehend these things with your heart, for that is where the release occurs. Open now and let me reveal the Truth. You are ready!

I will continue leading you on the path of the Three Enlightenments. Now that you have begun feeling the effects of the Emissary Wheel that awakens at a cellular level, you are ready to understand the path you have entered. The Wheel naturally contains everything I will share, so continue to meditate with it as often as you can. Do not direct the course of this meditation, but let it direct you. Simply gaze upon the geometry and let it pull you in. The rest, however glorious, will happen by itself. Over the next three days I will share more information regarding the Three Enlightenments. At this point it is still important to move between the soul and the mind with gentle ease, until the point comes when we will lay aside the mind for what will serve you more. There is nothing for you to fear in this. I am at your side and have walked this path before you. I will never lead you astray.

You have nearly made the final turn on the path that leads to your home, the place where the Beloved waits for you. I can feel the joy of my Father/Mother coming from that palace, for you have been away for a very long time.

—Brother

Lesson Thirteen

Are you ready to SEE the Door that opens before you, allowing you to step into "Your Truest Self"? This is the door you must pass through if you are to join me as a Spiritual Peacemaker. It has always been open, but your eyes have not. They have been closed, and you therefore thought the door was closed as well. But now you have progressed far enough to realize that there is nothing for you to fear, and no reason to remain blind. Open your eyes and step forward. I am waiting for you on the other side.

Your forgiveness is all that is required of you and is the path that leads to the First Enlightenment. But you must first release every idea you have ever had about what forgiveness is, otherwise it will not have the power to liberate you from the world you created in favor of the Real World. Liberation is required, for a master does not base his or her power in a world that does not exist. They seem to live in the world, just as you, but they are not of this world. Make no mistake about it – you have been called to do the same. You chose this path before you were born, the path of mastery, and now is the moment you must embrace it. A new definition of forgiveness must replace the old;

then you are ready. Then the door will pull you, rather than you having to exert any effort at all.

The First Enlightenment:

Illumined Mind

The Door that leads to the First Enlightenment is simply your willingness to forgive yourself. Until now forgiveness has been a concept in your mind, not a real experience. That is because you have perceived another person outside yourself that seems to need your forgiveness, and so you have ignored the real lesson, that which leads directly to the Illumination of your Mind. The possibility of "Perfect Unity" must first be accepted by your mind because you have given your mind so much power. The mind's power is extremely limited, but you have forgotten where your real source of power lies and have unknowingly bolstered the weakest part of you. And because the Holy Spirit would never deny you anything, it begins the process where you are, not where you are not. It uses the concepts you have accepted into your mind to ultimately release the concepts you have accepted into your mind. Did you understand that statement? We are using thought to release thought because you have given your thoughts so much value. Their value ultimately has no meaning outside of time, and therefore chains you here, blocking your awareness of what is true, your timelessness. And yet, there is nothing we cannot use to initiate the transformation that is required, even that which has no purpose at all.

There is only one statement you must learn and fully embrace to welcome the First Enlightenment. Repeat it over and over throughout the day, and every time you feel yourself entering into judgement.

"My perfect release comes from forgiving myself for what never occurred."

An Illumined Mind has directly experienced "Perfect Unity," not as a concept but as a real, tangible thing, and therefore has realized the futility of forgiving anything or anyone outside itself. There is nothing to forgive because there is no one outside you to forgive. (You will ultimately discover that this statement applies to you as well, for the concept of "you" is the only true hurdle to your awakening. But we must begin by drawing your attention inward, away from the world of form, the world where you seem to be vulnerable to attack.) You are experiencing the projections of your own split mind because it keeps you from taking full responsibility for everything that happens to you.

Forgiveness is the only path you must walk now, for it reveals everything you really desire. You are ready to lay down your sword and stop hurting yourself. Then the door swings wide and you enter with ease.

Perhaps it would be best for me to lay this step out as clearly as words will allow. If this seems to threaten you in any way, or shakes the foundation of the world you cling to now, then bless that experience and do not resist it at all. Your resistance will only lead to greater pain. Simply take a deep breath and allow everything, but open your heart to these truths. I am telling you these things because I care for you so deeply, and because of the agreement we made before time began. We agreed that we would work together to end all things of time in favor of the reality that cannot be threatened by any illusions. I intend to keep that agreement.

Do not try to understand these thoughts with your mind, but let your heart absorb them all:

> *The world you think you live in is not real.*
>
> *There is no one for you to forgive, including yourself, since your concepts of*

yourself are as unreal as the world you created to hide in.

You cannot hide forever.

God does not even know you are here. You are like a child that fell asleep and dreams. The child's parent sits beside him/her and will not move until the fever breaks. And yet there is no time in which the parent gives reality to what it knows doesn't exists.

Your fever is breaking now.

When you wake up from the dream the first question you will ask is: "Why did I keep my eyes closed for so long?"

This is the moment you chose to remember who you are. Nothing is important but this. Your forgiveness is the path that leads you to this moment.

Finally,

These thoughts, if you are willing to fully accept them into your mind, lead to the

First Enlightenment. Breathe them in, and you will realize peace at last.

—Brother

Lesson Fourteen

Your Mind is now Illumined and you have opened the first door that leads to the Truth within. You have done this by forgiving yourself for an offense that never occurred in reality, and have therefore seen past all the walls that seemed to separate you from the Real World. And though you will now be tempted to believe that you have finally achieved the goal established for you before time began, you must not stop. Though the new world you perceive with your Illumined Mind will appear in a light you could have never before imagined, your journey has only begun. Move forward and prepare your Heart for the next movement, for your Spirit dwells in this Sacred Chamber and needs to be released now. It is the next step, the second door, and you are ready to enter.

It is important that we define forgiveness so you will not be confused. I have said that you must forgive yourself, and others, for the offenses you perceived with your mind but which in reality never occurred at all. What does this mean? I have also said that your salvation comes naturally when you realize the difference between the world you made for yourself and the world made for you by God. The ego sees everything as separate and alone, waiting for death as if it was the natural ending to all things that live, and it created a world that reflects this decision. God knows that anything that lives at all lives forever, and that separation and isolation are impossible. Therefore, the world you presently perceive is directly opposed to the Real World, and must therefore be released before you can enter. Both cannot be real, and you are choosing which one you will see every moment. You can choose again whenever you want. Let this be the moment of your release, for delay is unjustified. If you knew the sacrifice you were making by denying the world God has made, then you wouldn't wait another second. Take my hand now, for I have seen both worlds and can show you the one where Love alone is real. It is not here, the place of separate bodies and broken dreams. And yet it is but a step away, a simple shift in your mind, then in your heart. That is the journey I am leading you on, and you can trust me not to lead you astray.

You are not bound by the laws of two worlds, but by the world you choose to SEE.

Ultimately only one is real, but both will "seem" real to a confused mind. Are you willing to accept that until now you have been confused? This acceptance is not meant to increase your guilt, but to end it. You are ready to release the world that never gave you what you really wanted, and accept a New World where all those things are already yours. Your willingness to lay aside one leads to your acceptance of the other, and the limitations that bound you in the first are then set aside. The world of bodies will not fade, but its effects will. Do you understand the difference? Until now you have been afraid that to accept the world God has prepared for you means you must leave behind all the things you love in this world. Nothing you love can ever be lost, for loss directly opposes love. The nature of love is gain, not loss. You will bring it all with you, and time cannot leave its deadly mark upon your soul. And yet, you will know that you are the Love you seek. It has always been yours and cannot change. You are that love, and it will never fade away.

The Second Enlightenment:

Awakened Heart

I would like to share a thought that has the power to undo all the illusions you have ever held about yourself and the world. If you accept it into your heart, and follow its inner promptings, then it will open the second door.

The Thought:

Your willingness to forgive others as you have forgiven yourself is the Door that leads to the Second Enlightenment.

Are you able to see how these two things exist together as a single Holy Action? Your mind opens when you realize that the sins you thought you committed have been forgiven already, and then your heart is awakened the moment you extend this gift to others. The love of God is a circle and must flow in every direction. Until now it has encompassed a narrow field, usually the one you inhabit moment to moment. Open your heart and give this gift freely, and then you will have it freely. There is only one way for you to keep this vital flow alive, and that is to share it. Forgiveness is the path, but seen in a new light, wholly free from the restraints of the ego's world. There is nothing for you to forgive now, and within this truth does your freedom lie, and the freedom of everyone you touch.

There are two things I would ask you to focus on for the next three days. The first is a simple formula that will help you understand how the Three Enlightenments work:

First the Mind surrenders, then SEES; next the Heart surrenders, then SEES; finally the Soul awakens, then KNOWS.

Meditate on this formula and you may begin to discover its simple design. All I can tell you now is that it is related to the code that has been inserted into each lesson in this course. I told you that these lessons are meant to activate your soul at different levels, both gross and subtle. This formula will bring these two closer than you can imagine.

And as often as you can these next few days, chant this single word: YES! You already know what it means and where it leads. Open to it now.

—Brother

Lesson Fifteen

The formula that was offered last week is a key that will help you understand, first intellectually, then in your soul, the process of enlightenment. We will leave our discussion on the Three Enlightenments for a moment while we enter into this more fully.

The Formula:

First the Mind surrenders, then SEES; next the Heart surrenders, then SEES; finally the Soul awakens, then KNOWS.

This formula applies both to the order in which you are experiencing enlightenment, as well as the method. Notice the way I expressed those words. I did not say, "the order in which you WILL experience enlightenment," for that would mean that it is not yours now, or that I am somehow different than you. There is nothing that is full in my mind that is not also complete in yours. I know this, and now it is time for you to know it as well. I have said that you are already awake, and the only difference between your mind and mine is that I believe these words fully. You have considered them, but it is not the same as realizing that any other thought would be impossible, especially now. It is who

73

you are, and I constantly look upon this reality. Open your eyes and you will do the same.

The first experience you must embrace over all others if you are to fully integrate these lessons is "Surrender."

Why is surrendering so important before your mind and heart can fully open? The reason you seem lost is because you have been fooled into believing that you can find the Light on your own, or that your mind alone is capable of establishing the path that will lead you home. If this were true then you would have done it a long time ago. The fact that you are experiencing time at all indicates that you are incapable of doing anything on your own. You need help. Eternity is still nothing more than a concept in your mind, not an experience. A concept is a belief and can never be substituted for the truth. The first step is to release the concept completely and to realize that you DO NOT KNOW THE PATH TO WALK. You cannot be shown where to go or how to proceed until you admit that you do not know. Then the path is illumined at your feet, and the memory of your home returns.

To the ego the statement, "I don't know," is a sign of weakness or failure. In reality it is the first step toward wisdom, and sets you firm upon the path of realizing your enlightenment. There is so much help that you can receive, but not until you surrender and admit that on your own you have failed. This is not because God wishes to ridicule you, but because you will not be able to fully embrace the truth until you realize that you are helpless on your own. Embracing the fact that you DO NOT KNOW THE PATH TO ENLIGHTENMENT is the only thing that the Holy Spirit needs to show you everything. It is like cracking a door open and letting the light stream in. The objects in the room that a moment before seemed dark and ominous, now appear as they really are – harmless projections of your sleeping mind. Let them go and they are gone, but you must surrender what you thought they were in order to be shown the truth.

The Mind cannot KNOW anything. This is reserved for the Soul. The Mind assumes and judges and all its judgments are based upon its past experiences. And because it places so much importance on the past, it seeks to make the future like it. It therefore drags its limited knowledge of everything like a weight into every experience, never once considering that the very premise of its thought system is insane. The present moment is never seen at all, for it is nothing more than a bridge that exists between the past and the future, hardly worth considering. The mind never realizes that resting for a moment in this Holy Instant could solve all its troubles. This is the most threatening thing in the whole universe to the ego, for it means that you have to admit that you never knew where to go, what to do, or anything at all. You are admitting that you are like a child, completely helpless. To the ego it means you failed and deserve nothing at all. In reality, it means that you are very near your greatest success.

Let the past go and do not consider the future at all; then the present moment will appear before you as a great beacon of light leading you to the place you never left except in your imagination.

Rest for a moment in the "I don't know" experience. Let it wrap around you like a warm blanket, keeping you free from all the empty snares of this world. It could be your salvation, if only you would allow it. There is nothing for you to fear when letting go could give you everything you desire. Nothing temporary will suffice now. The complete abandonment of the ego is the only thing that will lead you to where you really want to go.

The second word for you to consider in this formula is "SEE."

Your eyes were made not to see, or to see what isn't really there. The SEEING you are being led to is not a function of this world, but of the world reserved for you in eternity. When you open your spiritual eyes, which is what enlightenment really means, reality appears before you as it really is. You SEE what is there, instead of what never existed at all. Are you willing to consider that it is this simple? Are you willing to surrender everything you thought you saw a moment ago and SEE what has never changed?

—Brother

Lesson Sixteen

Today's lesson begins a gentle shift in focus. You are here because your soul is choosing to be a Spiritual Peacemaker. It may seem like you made this choice with your mind, or even with your heart. In reality it was made in both your mind and your heart, which then activated the place within your soul that IS this. We will now begin to explore this movement, the manner in which your soul chooses the experience it lives, and how you will integrate these three into one perfect extension of your Holiness and Grace.

You will also be offered ways to ground this awakening into your conscious Self, moving enlightenment from a concept in your mind to a reality you can know and live. Until now I have shared the concepts of the Illumined Mind, but they will not take us where we need to go. The Awakened Heart is the real first step, as it unites with the Mind. These two together present the final possibility, the full remembrance of your Divinity. We will not stop until we cross that final bridge and set your feet upon solid ground. Then you will not need these lessons, or anything this world can offer. Then you will KNOW that you are Home, and that all things are contained within that Perfect Light. You will not judge anything as right or wrong, good or bad, but will look upon it all with forgiving eyes. And your forgiveness will be whole, for there will be nothing left to block the radiant flow of the Beloved's Love as it washes you clean from all the broken promises you made yourself. You are that Love, and you are ready to embrace your Self and BE as God perceives you.

The Second Enlightenment:

You will not be close to fulfilling your role as a Spiritual Peacemaker until you have achieved the Second Enlightenment, Awakened Heart. Countless people have achieved the first level, and yet the energy of their Illumined Mind was not strong enough to catapult them past their illusions. The Illumination of your mind involves seeing what is in front of you every moment. It is a vast achievement because you have been spending all your time seeing what is NOT in front of you. Do you understand this now? Everything you thought was real was merely a shadow of the reality you are about to perceive. Seeing what is real and acting with Spiritual Integrity are not always compatible, however. The ego's grasp upon a person who has only achieved the First Enlightenment is still very strong, and without the empowered heart the temptation to use the new awareness for the ego's glorification will persist. That is why it is so important that you resist the urge to believe you have done anything at all. If you look around you and SEE what is real, that you are one with all beings and possess the power of that wholeness, do not consider it an accomplishment. Keep moving forward, into the heart, for only it is able to untie the knots that bind you to the ego's desire.

The Illumined Mind is achieved so simply. You have convinced yourself that it may take years of study and sacrifice, but it is not true. It is as easy as opening your eyes and admitting you were fooled before. I have already shared how important it is for you to joyfully accept the failure of your entire system of thought. Do not bemoan what has had no effect at all, but release it with eagerness and delight. Your goal isn't to be right, but to be happy once and for all. Being right in this world is such a limited frame, while happiness is a true gift from God. But it will not come to you until you admit that you were looking at shadows while the world of your dreams was lived just beyond your reach. This admission is the simple first step to the Illumination you have asked to receive. Once you admit you were wrong, then you can choose to see everything in a new way, the only way that reflects the truth you feel deep within your heart. Open your eyes and see what has always been real. There is no need to recreate the world, for your vain imaginings have never changed it at all. Your full and open gaze is all that is required now; then your Mind will spring into a new life.

You are now a single step away from bringing Peace to the world. You have learned to SEE what is true, now you must FEEL it as well.

I want to share a simple exercise that will help you prepare yourself for the initiation that lies ahead. You will likely immediately feel power in these words and actions. Practice them as often as you can, not only for the next three days but for the rest of this course. It is like a key that will open powerful energy centers within. The more you dedicate yourself to this exercise the more value it will hold.

If possible, do this at a time when you are very relaxed and at peace. You may choose to do it in the shower, or after you have prayed or meditated. When you have centered your mind, turn to your heart and let it open wide. The purpose of this exercise is to begin the process of FEELING who you are, and then knowing you are awake. Here is the exercise:

Wrap your arms around yourself and say these words over and over, meaning them with your whole heart:

"You are the awakened Heart."

Do not think about what this means with your mind, but with your heart. Think with your heart. There is a secret I could share with you about this chant, but I will wait until the next lesson. For now, only FEEL. And then, KNOW.

—Brother

Lesson Seventeen

Welcome again, Beloved Friends, to this dialogue on awakening. The words we speak are but the symbols of the Light we share, and it is this Light that leads you to the true goal, the Home you never left.

The dream of separation ends when you ask it to. What can this mean but that you have not yet asked it to end? Why? Because you were afraid of what might be waiting for you, what reward or punishment you may enjoy or despise. Your Brother's job is simply to report back to you what he has seen, and to remind you how safe it is to remember who you really are. I have seen the path that lies before you, for I have walked it just as you are walking it now. I too felt the pain of forgetfulness, but then the dawn of a new world flooded my heart, and I was able to see again. And now are you waking up, and your Brother takes you by the hand while the sleep still fills your eyes. I am here, and I will not leave you until our job together is done.

You have asked to become a Spiritual Peacemaker, and you are beginning to realize what that means. It does not require a sacrifice at all, unless you still believe that giving up what was never true is a sacrifice. You have come far enough to realize that the only thing that is real is Love itself, and all the loving extensions of your Healed Mind will come with you into the world God has prepared. You will bring peace by BEING Peace. That is why peace is not a function of this world, for true peace is impossible here. It is a function of the Real World, and that is where I am leading you to now. Open your eyes, Beloved Friend, and SEE what you have hidden from. There is no reason to be afraid now, for Love has come to greet you.

Last week's exercise was very important, for it was meant to give you a tangible experience of your Healed Mind. I asked you to wrap your arms around yourself and say these words with profound conviction: "You are the Awakened Heart." If you did this then you will have felt a movement that is impossible to describe. If you really meant these words, not with your mind but with your whole heart, then your life has changed.

Some of you may have wondered why I asked you to say, "You are the Awakened Heart," as opposed to, "I am the Awakened Heart." There is a very good reason. The real purpose of this exercise is to train you to become a Bridge to others, for that is the true function of a Spiritual Peacemaker. You are being led to imitate one of the most vital aspects of the Beingness of God. It is the Holy Spirit, and you are being led to this now. You are being called to be the physical counterpart of the Holy Spirit's function on earth. Do you feel how important this job is? Let's look for a moment at what this function is so you may understand the Holy Benefits of this exercise.

This is the moment you have been waiting for. The Holy Spirit's only job is to act as a bridge between the Real World and the world you are perceiving now. It speaks both languages, though it has not forgotten which is real and which isn't. Therefore, it is a gift to all who would remember the truth within them, for it reminds you that you are not at home here. It reinterprets the function of the world and reestablishes your role as Healer and Guide. Why? Because you will integrate this gift only by sharing it. Therefore, you are being asked to imitate the Holy Spirit's function, or in other words, to be the body, the mind, and the heart through which it expresses its only thought: "Only God's Will is True." This is why you were born, and it is the truest purpose of your life.

There is no difference between the "You" that you embraced through the last exercise, and the "You" you will embrace this week. They are the same, and you will be asked to FEEL them as the same from this moment on. Only then will you touch the heart of this gift, and begin to experience the Second Enlightenment – Awakened Heart.

At least three times in the next three days, find another person that you can serve. Here's all I ask of you – wrap your arms around them and say, either in your mind or out loud, "You are the Awakened Heart." Try to feel this energy in the same way you felt it before, when you were wrapping your arms around yourself. You may want to do that a few times before you extend this exercise so you can remember the feeling. You are saying the same words, and you are giving the same gift. There is no difference at all, and this is what you are trying to have a tangible experience of. Practice this as often as you can. This will test the level of seriousness you bring to this course. I cannot overemphasize the importance of this, because without the experience I am leading you to here, all these things will only be concepts in your mind. As I said before, concepts in your mind, even if they are illumined, will not help you now. Your heart must now FEEL what you know in your mind. Then you are ready to move into the Third Enlightenment – Realized Soul.

These were the lessons I offered my friends two thousand years ago, and only a few were able to integrate them. But now there is enough energy present, and enough people have walked this path at my side, to allow you to enter.

—Brother

Lesson Eighteen

You are undergoing an intense training, though you may not realize where it is leading you. You have asked to become a Spiritual Peacemaker, but it is still impossible for you to understand what this means. It is very different than the world's idea of peace or how that can be accomplished. This is already clear to you. Your eyes are beginning to open to the reality we are seeking, but they are still only half open. You are seeing two worlds at once, one of imagined dreams where you created a world built upon an impossible foundation, and the world where you can clearly SEE the truth that never changes. You may find yourself moving between these two worlds without even knowing it, for the differences are often subtle and hard to perceive. But they will soon become more obvious, and you will not be able to deny the truth any longer. Soon your eyes will open wide, and the world of dreams will disappear completely. Then you will KNOW what it means to bring peace, not with your mind but your whole Self. Then you will be a true servant of humanity, of reality, and everything will make perfect sense to you.

We are going to stay with the Second Enlightenment for one more lesson before we move forward. There is a step we must take together before we can consider the Third; otherwise it will be nothing more than a concept, not a real experience. The Awakened Heart is where we must devote most of our attention because it is where the real foundation lies. Achieving the First Enlightenment is significant but nowhere near the goal, and the Third Enlightenment occurs on its own, without any effort at all, once you have fully opened to the Second. You have come a long way, but there is a step you must take now that you cannot take on your own. That is why I am here, for this is function of an Enlightened Guide.

In the last two lessons you were asked to first embrace yourself as the Awakened Heart, and then embrace another in the same way, knowing that it is the same. The "You" you embraced does not change simply because the frame of reference is different. In other words, the ego believes that because you are more intimately aware of your own self, symbolized by the body, it must surely be different than the self of the other. It sees through your eyes, not theirs, and therefore builds a solid case for its theology of separation. What it does not remember is that it made the body for this very purpose, and claims it still. It has forgotten that the Vision of God extends past all bodies and form and claims them as one. Therefore, when you claim the Awakened Heart within anyone, whether it be yourself or a person who seems to be separate from you, you are the one claiming it.

Is this beginning to make sense? This is what we mean when we say, "It is in giving that we receive." *What I give to thee is received by me*. And though you have begun to understand and even experience this truth, it is still like a fog in your mind. It is for this reason that you have been given a Master Teacher, one who has cleared the mist that claims you now, and can hold your hand while you do the same. Your Teacher is not here to stand above or beyond where you claim to be, but to simply create a bridge between your mind and heart, much as you are becoming a bridge to others. When seen in this Light then the function begins to make perfect sense. Your Teacher has not come to take anything away from you, but to help you claim everything you thought you lost.

I am within you now, alive and open, ready to show you the heart that loves the world. It does not matter whether you claim my personality as your guide, or the personality of another. It is all the same and makes no difference at all. But you must at this point reach out your hand and ask for help. There is a subtle shift that needs to take place in your heart now, and it will not occur if you convince yourself that you have come further than you actually have. The Teacher appears to lead you home, so that you may in turn offer the same to those that will be given to you.

The Teacher asks you to SEE through his or her heart, not your own. Your heart is not open enough to contain the Light that would flood your being the moment you fully surrender. That is why the first role of one who has achieved the Third Enlightenment is to be a bridge to those who walk behind them. I can offer you the only bridge you need, and yet it is not about any particular identity. The nature of the final stage in your awakening is that you will no longer identify yourself as different from any other being— in particular, other beings that are also awake. Turning toward the Buddha nature within is the same as turning toward your Christ Consciousness. Each is a reference, nothing more, which will link your mind to the eternal movement of Spirit that flows through us all. We are the same in this, and this is the purpose of the bridge I offer.

For the next three days, look through my heart often. Consciously see the world and everything you experience as if I am the one experiencing all of it, not you. When you cross this bridge and reach the other side, then you will see that we are the same, that we share the same heart. Then you will KNOW and you will SEE. The next step will then be yours.

—Brother

Lesson Nineteen

We stand together on a bridge so sacred that words can never describe the grace we feel. We will stop and consider this final step for a moment, the journey from one holy thought to another, from the place you never left to the home where you have always lived. Your mind wandered away for a moment, but your Spirit has always remained, and we will rejoin it now with the awareness of your Illumined Mind and Awakened Heart. This is the only thing that has been lacking, your awareness of who you have always been, but now even that fades into the ocean of timelessness. Nothing has been lost, and all thoughts of separation dissolve into the Holy Vision you now perceive. One final step and you are there. Take my hand, and I will lead you into the safety of your Sacred Self.

I want to describe the single action of this final step, what we are calling "Realized Soul." It is the Third Enlightenment, and you already possess the fruits of this gift, though until now you have closed your eyes to them all. As we stand together on this Bridge of Awakening, I will share the single lesson that will mean more than all the rest, and yet it is the one your mind will be most unwilling to grasp. That is because this

Holy Action is so foreign to its current system of thought, that which separates everything from itself. If you can lay aside this resistance, even for a moment, and enter into this current like a child, then your Realized Soul will dawn, and you will remember all the things you once tried to forget.

Open now and try to understand what I will now describe.

A fully Realized Being moves through all worlds with one word, one thought and one feeling surrounding their heart. This word is the bridge we have been discussing. Though a thousand words move through their space, there is only one that is heard. Though a million thoughts enter their mind then leave, only one remains. And though their feelings may change as all emotions change, there is one that remains full and real. I will describe this as a single word, though even this word does not approach the Holy Altar I am offering to you now. If you can access the Light that lies behind the word, and then KNOW that you are that Light, then you will realize with your soul what may have seemed hidden for a time, but which has always been right in front of you.

YES!

Are you surprised? Did you expect a word you have never heard before, one with mystical powers you can never understand with your mind? I am telling you now that this word does have mystical powers you cannot understand with your mind. What I am asking is that you allow it to rest alone, isolated from all other words and thoughts for a moment, and see what magic it holds. If you do, then you will see that it is the only word you will ever need, though your mouth will continue to speak so many more, and your mind will race with other thoughts. Still, at the very center of it all, this one reality will exist, and it will pull you into an experience no word or thought can ever propel. Though you may speak a hundred million other words, they will all spring from the experience of YES! Though you will think an unthinkable number of thoughts, still will your YES be at the center of them all. And though your actions will vary from one moment to the next, they will not escape the YES that motivates them all.

When an enlightened being speaks, every word is YES. When they think, every thought is YES. When they act, every action is YES. And now as we stand together on this bridge preparing for this final step, I see this YES moving through you, acting as you, motivating every movement of your soul. This is the only thing you need to know, not with your conscious mind, for it will never be able to grasp what I am saying to you now. But there is a place that has been prepared, and you have been breathing life into this place from all the other lessons and thoughts we have shared. From this place will your YES awaken, and then you will fully grasp what I am saying to you.

In the next lesson I will offer several ways for you to access the Gift of this experience. In this lesson I have offered it as a concept, but as we have said so many times before, a concept will not help you now. It is like swimming at the surface of the ocean when all the treasures you seek lie far below. We are preparing to dive to that sacred chamber where the pearl of highest wisdom is sleeping. As it awakens, so will you. But you must be ready to leave the surface, and I believe you are ready. All the words you have spoken till now, all the thoughts and actions that have defined your life, have not given you what you really want. But this word, YES, radiating through them all, will show you that you have always had what you always wanted. Do you understand that this is the real goal we have set for ourselves, to KNOW that you have possessed this Holy Gift from the beginning of time? Nothing else matters now. Nothing will satisfy you but the Realized Soul you are about to enter.

Lay aside all your idle dreams and let them pass away from you. I have told you that nothing real will be threatened in this transition from illusions into reality. You will bring all your loving thought with you, for love itself is the only reward you will receive.

—Brother

Lesson Twenty

I have said that a master who has attained the Third Enlightenment, Realized Soul, lives within the Eternal Yes. What better advice could I give to you? If there were only one gift I could give, a single reward you would value over all others, it would be this word, this experience, this Holy Offering that has the power to transform the whole world. Live within the YES! I cannot tell you how to do this, for this gift is revealed to each one of us in its own unique way. All I can tell you is that the gift is before you now, and you have the power within to activate it. Choose it above everything else and it is yours. Do not wait another moment.

The first step in living within the Eternal Yes is realizing all the ways you have lived within the experience of "no." This is demonstrated by the ego's insistence that it is "not" everything. The whole universe conspires to reveal the truth to you, and yet you cling to the walls of your sleeping mind and say, "I am not That." The ego refuses to clearly identify what "That" is, for it knows in its heart that all questions would be answered within this Holy Light. The Spirit of Truth says, "You are That," and then proceeds in showing you what that means. The Spirit begs you to look around at the gifts of the universe and then tells you, "You are not separate from any of them." It looks upon the Highest of the High, and the Lowest of the Low, and it says to you, "You are all of That." Thus was YES born, and thus does it live within you now, if only YOU would live within IT now.

This is the beginning and the end of this course on Spiritual Peacemaking. I have saved this simple lesson for a time when all the other concepts and thoughts would be already before you, and after your heart and mind were opened sufficiently enough to accept the most essential teaching I can offer. Let your whole being claim the YES that is at the very core of your being. You are not here to reject anything, but to claim it all. This is what God does, and it is time for you to begin imitating God. You are ready for this, whether you realize it consciously or not. I would not have called you here if you were not ready, and if we had not made an ancient agreement to stand together in this Light. The YES of your soul has been ignited, and it sings to the whole world the Song of Remembrance.

I would like to offer two images to help you understand, and even practice, claiming the YES of your being.

Imagine yourself standing straight with your arms open. (For better effect, do this physically after you have read the descriptions.) Begin chanting the word YES over and over, and as you do, feel the energy of this word filling you. Now move your hands in an outward motion, as if you are giving this energy to others. Every time you say the word YES, push the Light away from your heart. Let it extend from you completely.

Now we will change the meditation to reflect how you have lived your life till now. (I do not mean to discredit you in any way by saying this, but it is important for you to know and embrace the guidance that has come from your ego, guidance which until now you have chosen to heed.) Begin chanting the word NO, and as you do, pull the energy toward your body. Every time you say the word NO, sweep the energy in toward you as if you are not willing to share it.

Now we will examine the meaning of this meditation. It was not a metaphor as much as a clear illustration of what you do in spirit whenever you make any decision at all. Ultimately, every decision or choice is a choice between YES, and NO. Do you see this clearly? When you live within the YES, the natural movement is to give away the same gift you have chosen to receive. The natural action of YES is expansion, whereas the natural action of NO is retraction. NO seeks to hide within its projections while YES chooses to give so that it may receive more. God is constantly giving, and so must you give everything if you are to "Be as God." The Divine does not hold back; therefore, it does not understand the experience of NO. Give all to have all. This is the true path to enlightenment.

If you changed the order, it would also provide a powerful lesson. Imagine that when you chant the word YES you are pulling the energy in toward yourself, and when you chant the word NO you push it away. In this example, the energy of YES seeks to contain all reality within itself, while the energy of NO seeks to project it onto others. YES takes full responsibility for everything it perceives, while NO takes no responsibility. The second experience chooses to reject itself by rejecting others. Thus does it find itself isolated and alone, while the whole world rotates around its center.

Find as many ways as you can in the next three days to live within the YES. This is one of the most valuable tools I can offer, for it is in living this that it becomes real to you. Be aware of the ways you are currently saying NO to the universe. Allow a new vision to take hold, one where YES is the only reality you embrace. Chant the word over and over. Clap your hands together, or pat all over your body in order to ground the experience. I am asking you to join me in the Eternal YES. Please answer.

—Brother

Lesson Twenty One

Today we begin our course again. Until now we have been laying the foundation upon which an amazing temple will be built. The foundation of any building is the most important step, and so it is with us, those seeking to be called "Instruments of Peace," "Emissaries of Light," or "Spiritual Peacemakers." The stones we have been laying upon the ground are the holy concepts of peace, grace, and the truth that cannot be challenged by anything you have made in this world. Now they are in place, and now we will progress into the very temple we have fashioned together.

You must now make a very important decision. Will you choose to rededicate yourself to this goal, after so many weeks and so many lessons? Will you decide this moment to increase your commitment that you may leave the world altogether and realize yourself to be what you have chosen to seek? You cannot complete your role unless you do this, for until now we have allowed a certain ease in our lessons. That moment has now passed, and it is time for you to decide once and for all if you are willing to take the final step toward full realization, and thus full service. You are ready, but will you choose?

If the answer within your soul is the "YES" we have been asked to live, then step forward. If there is any part of you that still believes you are not ready, then wait here for awhile and I will send angels to pick you up and lead you forward. You will not be left behind. I will see to that. Such a thing is impossible at this point, for I have called you to my side and you have answered. I am here and I will not leave. Take a deep breath, and take the step toward life.

There are only thirteen lessons left, and we will use them wisely. As I said, we have given you the tools, and now you must activate and use them. The final lessons will take everything we have learned till now and bring them together into a harmonious whole. We will take each of the twelve attributes of an Emissary of Light and we will apply them to the Three Enlightenments. Through this you will learn to ascend with them, as they ascend with you, to the holy altar of the temple we build together. For the next twelve lessons we will take each of the attributes and apply them to this template. On the thirteenth lesson we will be left with one final step, the step into your enlightened mind, heart and soul. We will also apply the central teaching, noted through the center triangle in the Emissary wheel, which is the foundation of our practice which: Surrender, Trust and Gratitude. (Have the image of the wheel near you as you read these final lessons.) The stage has been set. This is the moment you have been waiting for.

Remember: YOU ARE READY!

The First Attribute: Courage

The First Enlightenment, Illumined Mind:

Courage must first awaken in your mind before it can be felt in the world. It is this feeling that will ultimately lead to your release, but it must first be known as a possibility, however dim. As you awaken this enlightenment, it will become more real to you, and it will no longer be a concept. This is when you will know that a shift is beginning to occur, the shift into the Second Enlightenment. Hold this thought high in your mind, then, and know that there is nothing for you to fear. You are protected more than you know.

Surrender Meditation:

I surrender all those places within my mind that were afraid to step into my chosen role of being a Spiritual Peacemaker, and I acknowledge that only Divine Courage can lead me forward from here. I do not know what to do, but through my surrender I will be shown. I am that Courage now, fully Illumined.

The Second Enlightenment, Awakened Heart:

I now FEEL courage escape my Mind and release the power of my Awakened Heart. I am not waiting for this courage to dawn, but claim it now with energy and commitment. I am no longer afraid to fulfill my part in God's plan for salvation. My courage spills into the world now from my heart, and is seen and felt by all beings everywhere. My heart is sufficient unto all, and knows only the Light that leads it forward. I embrace courage and draw it inward, then extend it as a blessing to the world.

Trust Meditation:

I trust that you are with me now, Beloved One, and therefore I have the courage to step forward. There is no path I will walk that you have not already covered, and so I trust you and am filled with an inner strength that the world does not understand. I trust that you know the path to walk, and so I am courageous. I am that Courage now, fully Awakened.

The Third Enlightenment, Realized Soul:

My soul rejoices in the courage I have found within. My soul knows only this joy, for it exists only for this moment, the moment when courage propels me into my Divine Purpose of a Spiritual Peacemaker. I realize now why I was born into this world, and I will not waste another moment.

Gratitude Meditation:

I am grateful for the courage born within me today. My soul does now embrace this moment, for it is the moment I have waited for since I was created. I step forward in courage and I KNOW who I am, thus do I know all things. There is nowhere I need to go but where I am NOW. There is nothing I need do but what I am doing NOW. I am grateful for the courage I find within my soul. I am that Courage now, fully Realized.

—Brother

Lesson Twenty Two

The Second Attribute: Patience

The First Enlightenment, Illumined Mind:

Only eternal patience will bring immediate results. That is because eternal patience does not seek anything except what it already has, and it recognizes that it lacks nothing. Therefore, what comes from God remains with God, and it knows itself as God. There is nothing that can invade the deep peace this thought inspires, which comes from the Illumined Mind. It does not look to the physical world to prove its conviction, but to the Spirit where all things are given and received. You need nothing, and your recognition of this fact is your salvation.

There is nothing you can gain that you do not already possess in your soul, for all things exist and remain where you exist and remain. Therefore, they are already together. Do you see how simple this is? Your ego would have you believe that you must gain what you do not have, while your Spirit tells you that there is nothing that is not already yours. Which will you believe? Whose voice will you listen to, the voice of lack that comes from your ego, or the Voice of Peace that tells you the Truth? When you grasp this Truth then you will understand the real meaning of Patience; then you will be ready to sink into the Second Enlightenment.

Surrender Meditation:

I open my hands to receive all the gifts my Spirit wills for me. Until now my fist has been closed and I have been unwilling to surrender to the Divine Current that flows through me now. I accept that I made a mistake, and yet it has had no consequence at all. I let go and accept a new frame of reference, one where my surrender reveals all things that are already minc. I patiently accept all these gifts and know that they are fully revealed through and as me. Patience is the gift I give and receive. I am that Patience now, fully Illumined.

The Second Enlightenment, Awakened Heart:

Now that you KNOW that eternal patience is the only thing that will give you the immediate results you seek, you must begin to FEEL this completion. I say completion because it is what I perceive in you, and I am asking you to perceive the same. Your mind has accepted this, and now your heart must awaken to the reality I am describing. It is the only way for you to enter into the stream of Grace that a Spiritual Peacemaker must know and embrace in order to be of true service. Otherwise you will understand what you do not have, but this still leaves us far from our goal. Your ego will endure your understanding, but not your experience. This is where the real release takes place. But what the ego considers a battle you will turn around and see as a victory. As you patiently open to the Peace that has always been yours, the ego's defenses will fall on their own. No battle will ensue, for you have seen past it altogether.

I have been patient with you, and now you must be patient with yourself. Some of you wonder if you have been integrating the code I have placed within these lessons, for you have not been able to access it intellectually. I ask only that you look to the world around you and see how it has been healed. Be patient a moment longer and all your questions will be answered. I have chosen you for a reason, and now you must trust that I know what I am doing.

Trust Meditation:

I open my heart and Trust you, Beloved One, for you have not let me lose track of my Divine Purpose here on Earth. I have been given a Holy Guide to show me the path I walk, and I trust that my feet are being led toward the only goal worthy of my soul. I will be patient and let all things be revealed. The only thing that is required of me this moment is my trust, and I offer it now. I trust that the Universe is perfectly revealed through my Awakened Heart, and all things flow toward God. I am that Patience now, fully Awakened.

The Third Enlightenment, Realized Soul:

The immediate results you are seeking are already yours. What more do you need to hear? Realizing this, it should be a simple thing for you to be truly patient and Know that you have everything you need. In this way do we back into patience, for it is not a result we seek, but the very means through which we realize the truth. It is within your soul now, protected and whole. The more you access this Divine Patience, the more conscious it will become for you. Take a deep breath, then, and Know who you are. In doing so, you will know all things.

It is impossible for my words to ever fully describe this step, for it is not aligned with the world you have created in any way. It operates according to the laws of a different world, and your patience is the only thing that will lead you into it NOW. Decide this moment if it is what you really want. There is no sacrifice that will be required of you, except all your illusions. But if you are honest with yourself you will realize that they have never given you what you really want. Be free, then, and do not expect too much of a world that you designed to keep you from this truth.

Gratitude Meditation:

Patience has opened a new door for me to see who I am, and I am grateful for this gift. The only words that escape from my lips this day are – "Thank you my Beloved." At last I have realized who I am, and who I will always remain. I am that Patience now, fully Realized.

—Brother

Lesson Twenty Three

The Third Attribute: Wisdom

The third attribute that you must consciously integrate in choosing to join me as a Spiritual Peacemaker, is Wisdom. It is the fruit of the first two, Courage and Patience. The Wisdom you are seeking will reveal a new world to you, or a very old one. This is the world that has been prepared for you since the beginning of time. It is your rightful home, the place where you sleep even now. I am there with you holding your hand, and I will not leave your side until your eyes open and you are wide awake again. The Wisdom being offered to you now is the key to this moment. Will you take it from me, and from all the others who hold it safe for you?

I would like to lead you through a process of inquiry that will help you integrate this even further. I do this because I have accepted my role as a teacher and a healer, the same role you are choosing to accept this moment. Follow me, then, and see where this process leads. It ultimately leads nowhere at all, but you cannot realize this until you walk with me for just a moment. In that sacred moment will you know the truth, that there is no journey, no distance and no destination. You are walking to You, nowhere else, and you are ready to realize this now.

What is "Wisdom" but the full and combined Knowing of the mind, heart and soul? This is the path we have been walking together, is it not? Therefore, what is it you seek to Know? You are seeking the Truth, only the Truth. And what is the Truth you seek? It is simply that you are safe and invulnerable. But how can this be true if you exist in a world where you are anything but safe, where you experience possible peril in every moment? Remember that either the world's position or God's is true, but not both. Either you are vulnerable or you are safe. If you are choosing to listen to the Spirit within you, to know in your mind, heart and soul that you are safe, then could the world's version of reality be anything but false? Do you see this now? What can that mean but that the world you perceive is not real? But there must be another world that you can access and enjoy this very moment. It is the Heaven within, and it is with you now. You need do nothing but accept this rapture; then you will experience it. It is now, and it is yours. This is the essence of the Wisdom that this attribute describes.

The First Enlightenment, Illumined Mind:

The Wisdom that comes to the mind cannot be understood by the mind. This is because Wisdom is not bound by the laws of this world, and even your Illumined Mind is not completely divorced from these laws. It stands with one foot in the world of form and the other out. That is why I have said that accomplishing this level is nothing at all. It is only a step in the right direction, though a big step. Until Wisdom falls into the heart, then it is not full, and this, after all, is what you are seeking.

Surrender Meditation:

I surrender to the Wisdom I Know is within me. Where else would it be as it is revealed in my mind that opens now? And yet I will not hesitate. I will move forward into the Light that reveals the full rapture of this experience. I will step forward into the Holy Presence that the Beloved reveals within me now. I am that Wisdom now, fully Illumined.

The Second Enlightenment, Awakened Heart:

The Wisdom that comes to the heart can be understood, but not according to my former concepts or beliefs. These have only clouded what my heart has sought to reveal, and I let them pass now as a mist does clear when morning breaks. My heart ascends with this Wisdom, for it knows it well. It has slept within its deepest chamber waiting for this moment, and now that it is here, it rejoices. Wisdom is revealed, and I welcome it wholly.

Trust Meditation:

If I am to welcome this Light, then I must trust what it reveals. The shadows that once frightened me are seen and dispelled, for they were nothing but the images I created and held apart from love. Now I let them go, and I welcome what Wisdom reveals. I am that Wisdom now, fully Awakened.

The Third Enlightenment, Realized Soul:

Wisdom is nothing more than the realization in my mind and heart of what my Soul has always known. My Soul is the sacred sanctuary where the truth within me has been held safe. The Truth is who I am, and so I am the One that has been protected there. I am opening to see and Know this, and so I claim my enlightenment. What else could enlightenment be but this Holy Knowledge, integrated through me and as me? I am open to receive, and my openness is the only gift I need offer the Beloved. I am here, and so is God.

Gratitude Meditation:

I open in gratitude now, for the truth has come, and I have welcomed that truth. My heart explodes with the love that has always been contained there, and fills the sky with such Light that my former self simply falls away, revealing the Sacred Self where I make my home. I fall into the refreshing waters of Soul Realization, and everything I have ever sought is found, and every question I have ever asked is answered. I claim this because it is my right as the Holy Child of God. I hold it in my hand with the same tenderness that the Beloved once held me while I slept. I am that Wisdom now, fully Realized.

— Brother

Lesson Twenty Four

You are journeying toward the center of the Wheel, and as you move through the spokes away from the outer edge you begin to feel something falling away from you. What is leaving you are the thoughts you have held of yourself that have never served the Divine Purpose for which you were created. Let them pass you by happily, for you do not need them any longer.

The only thing you need is to remember an ancient agreement you made before you were born, even before the thought of birth in this world seemed possible. That moment is not so far away as you might think; in fact, it is happening right now. That is why the ending is sure, that you will awaken and fulfill this Holy Contract. That is why I am so confident in the Light that draws you forward, for I am standing before the transformed YOU now. If you want you can sense me there, holding you and loving the truth within that was never changed by your meaningless dream. We look upon each another in gratitude for the One that made our dreams of separation impossible, and never allowed us to fall too deeply into the snares of a world that never existed.

Your journey to the center of the Emissary Wheel is simply your willingness to REALIZE and to KNOW what God perceives in you, and in realizing this will the contract be fulfilled. For then you will extend this blessing, which is as natural as your breathing. Others will remember, and they will know through you. This is why you have answered the call to be a Spiritual Peacemaker. Nothing else will satisfy you now. All other pleasures will seem vain compared to this. And thus it should be, for the Light has entered your Heart.

The Fourth Attribute: Certainty

We will now speak of the gift of Certainty, which you are realizing now. I have said that the path to enlightenment is simply the movement away from Faith, through Certainty, and finally into Realization. Faith is of the Illumined Mind, the intellectual understanding that only love is real. It is not until you are certain, which springs from the Awakened Heart, that your transformation is secured, and then finally Realized in your Soul. Do you see how simply this transition takes place? First you believe, then you feel, then you know. And yet it would be incorrect to conclude that enlightenment does not occur until the final stage of Knowingness is experienced, for that would mean that God's Vision of you can be changed by your vision of yourself. That is not possible, and it is this fact that ultimately secures your release from hell. Hell is in your mind, and cannot leave the home you have created for it. When your Mind is Illumined, and your Heart is Awakened, then hell has no place at all in your Realized Soul.

If you are to attain the Certainty I am describing to you now, you must be willing to ask yourself one simple question. This question, if answered well, is all you need to open this Fourth Attribute, diving even closer to the center of the Wheel where all answers are revealed.

*If you could only be certain of one thing in
this world, one thing only, what would it be?*

I am confident that the first answer that came to your mind was Love. "Only the Love of God is real." If this is true, and if reality cannot be threatened by illusions, then we have found ourselves at a Divine Junction. What is real cannot be threatened, and only God's love is real. What does that mean? It means that you can leave behind all things that do not serve this end, and enter the sacred chamber where LOVE lives NOW. It is waiting for you, just as you have waited for it. Enter now, and SEE for yourself.

The First Enlightenment, Illumined Mind:

There is no place where the experience of Certainty and your mind meet. I have said to you many times that this first Illumination is only the first step of your enlightenment. You cannot be content with the Light it reveals, though it may at first seem very bright indeed. Acknowledge it and move on, for there is so much more to come. The mind can only believe; it cannot Know. Certainty is the same as Knowing.

Surrender Meditation:

I remain where I have been, and I surrender all these thoughts to you, Beloved One. I live in the Divine "not-knowing" even as my mind is illumined by the Light that extends past this world. I will not stay here for long, for Certainty calls me, and I will answer. I am that Certainty now, fully Illumined.

The Second Enlightenment, Awakened Heart:

It is here that Certainty finds its home, for what the heart feels, it can realize. This is the Gift you have been searching for, for the feeling that Love inspires washes away the stains of forgotten dreams. The dream is ending now, and you are ready to take the final step.

Trust Meditation:

What can I say now, Beloved? I Trust the direction you are leading me, for I feel what will soon be revealed. I know that we have come too far to retreat, for the past is receding and falling away. Only Love remains, and I am certain that you are here. I am that Certainty, fully Awakened.

The Third Enlightenment, Realized Soul:

Of this we cannot speak. No concept, no matter how holy it may seem, can cross this boundary, for the mind and even the heart have been replaced with something far more essential. Just breathe, and Know that you have made it Home.

Gratitude Meditation:

Through Gratitude is my Certainty revealed. Say this over and over. Feel the fruit of this Divine Light now. It is the only gift you need. I am that Certainty now, fully Realized.

—Brother

Lesson Twenty Five

The Fifth Attribute: Compassion

All beings strive to be released from bondage. It is the most natural urge within the soul, even when it is clouded and obscured by the selfish desires that seem to block its return to grace. Knowledge of the Higher-Self is inherent within the mind of the lower-self, which stretches for what it cannot fully comprehend. Every cell in every body holds the blueprint of the "Realized Master," and that is why nothing of this world will ever satisfy the larger part of you. Your lower-self follows every road that seems to offer satisfaction or release, yet its motto is "seek but never find." And yet, you have discovered a new path, one that leads away from the empty promises of this world, and you will not be denied the gift you seek. Compassion has brought you here, and it will give you everything you need to fulfill your heart's desire.

The gift of "Divine Compassion" is the result of Certainty, which you have already achieved. I say that you have already achieved it because this is what I see in you. I refuse to acknowledge the part of you that still believes it has anything left to do or to achieve before this experience is yours. I look upon what is whole in you, not what seems to be lacking, and when you learn to do the same, then the lack will disappear on its own. No effort is required to dispel an illusion, but it takes great effort indeed to deny what is and has always been true. This is why your heart is so tired, because you have used the power of creation to deny the power of creation. Do you see this, Beloved? When you release and let go of this insane need, then you will no longer feel this dis-ease. Then will Compassion reign in your soul, for you will have extended your Certainty to the world and beyond.

Compassion is the act of extending your Certainty to others. It is that simple. Once your spiritual eyes have opened and you are able to See what has always been right in front of you, then you will KNOW who you are. But this is not a stagnant knowledge. It must continue to flow, just as the Love of God flows, in order for your eyes to remain open. The moment you stop giving what you have freely received, your eyes will close again and you will return to the world of separating dreams. But if you are able to give what you know you are, then you will remain awake, and be a blessing to all.

This is your simple role as a Spiritual Peacemaker, to give what you know yourself to BE. It does not mean that you are here to change the world, or to change anyone in the world, but to set it all free. Freedom is what is required, for all beings sense the bondage of this world, and seek to be released from it. You are the point of release for yourself, and yet all other points intersect with yours. The Art of Spiritual Peacemaking and the Art of Compassion are therefore the same.

Compassion is the most natural experience to those who are awake, because they would never choose to attack themselves. They know that every action or word is directed at the source of their experience, and knows itself to be that source. Why, then, would they choose to offer what would limit, when they could instead give what would release? This choice is always before you, and that is why we say that the Kingdom of Heaven is before you as well. It is here now, in the next decision you make or the next word you say. Is that so hard for you to believe, that Heaven could be so close? It is, but only if you choose to See it, and you will See it if you Give it to All.

The First Enlightenment, Illumined Mind:

Compassion is reasonable to the mind because it is easy to see where it leads. It can only lead to harmony because it seeks to unite rather than divide. Therefore, it does not compete with reality but establishes it where it belongs.

Surrender Meditation:

I let go of my need to understand what I must do, what I must say, or where I must go, and accept Compassion as my only guide. It cannot lead me astray, and so I surrender to everything it reveals. I will be as a child and not assume I have the answer, and in doing so will a new answer dawn upon my mind. I am that Compassion now, fully Illumined.

The Second Enlightenment, Awakened Heart:

The Awakened Heart is perfectly aligned with Compassion, for it is not confused about its role in bringing peace. It can only come through union, and so they are the same.

Trust Meditation:

I am willing to trust everything Compassion shows me, for its vision of peace is so much clearer than mine. I know that the more I trust, the more I will see, and this is my only goal now – to see what is real. I am that Compassion, fully Awakened.

The Third Enlightenment, Realized Soul:

Compassion has lost its purpose now, for in the end it is only the bridge into the state of Perfect Knowing. Now that I stand on the other side of this river, the bridge is no longer useful to me. I let it pass with gratitude and joy.

Gratitude Meditation:

How can I express my gratitude for the gift of new life? I have crossed into a world where only love is real, and yet I have not moved at all. I will stand here for a moment and extend this gratitude to the One that has brought me to the Home I never left except in my imagination. I am that Gratitude now, fully Realized.

—Brother

Lesson Twenty Six

The Sixth Attribute: Joy

Many have claimed to hear the Voice for God and to record messages they have received. There was a time when many of my words were recorded, and they were said to have come from God. Know that it is true, that every word that has come from my mouth has been from God. But it is no different for you, when you allow yourself to be used by the Spirit and the Way of God. This, as you know, is your goal.

I was once quoted as saying: "I have come to give you life so that your joy will be complete." It would be more accurate if this were as follows: "I have come to give you back to Life so that your joy may be perfect." This is what we will explore today, Beloved One, for you are at last ready to lay aside all the ways you have limited your joy and convinced yourself that you were satisfied. You may have believed this in your mind, but not in your heart or soul. That is why I've stressed the importance of the Second and Third Enlightenments over the First. Even when you realize with your mind that your joy has never been complete, and you know that you deserve this gift, it is not enough momentum to catapult you into Perfect Joy. This is why I have come, and it is where you will go so that the others who follow you will recognize the gift they too deserve. Isn't this the real mission of a Spiritual Peacemaker, to demonstrate that Perfect Joy is the beginning and the end of our search for God and enlightenment? Isn't this the reason you came to this place, to learn how to lay aside all the things of this world that have robbed you of the gift given by your Divine Parent? But now you have come far enough to realize this and to act upon it, and as always, you will have it by giving it to others.

You have allowed yourself to become completely Certain of one thing, that you are loved by God. From that love has come the gift of extension through Compassion, which is the art of sharing what has been given to you by God. Now we enter the third Attribute in this triad: Joy. Now that you have realized love and given love to all, Perfect Joy is released. How natural is this release when your heart and soul open! It is a sense that cannot be described by any definition this world holds dear.

Perfect Joy is ultimately the realization of your invulnerability, or that the world of form is not real and cannot attack or hurt you. Do you see how we keep coming back to this place? If Perfect Joy is to reign then you must make peace with this fact. The world you see with your eyes is not the same world you experience with your soul. It is only a reflection of the decisions you have made about yourself, all the ways you have tried to hide from the Truth within you. But you cannot hide any longer. You have come outside the cave too far, and you have seen what the ego never intended for you to see. Now it is only a matter of time before the whole Matrix of Illusion falls on its own, for you have seen behind the curtain, and you know what is really happening. This is the beginning of mastery, for you cannot be a master of something you cannot control. And you cannot control the world unless you made it. Herein lies the gift of peace, and Perfect Joy is sure to follow.

The First Enlightenment, Illumined Mind:

You are being asked to See the world as God Sees it, as a reflection of your beliefs. Now that you realize this, you can choose to see in a new way. The "Way of Grace" will lead you, and you will experience the Joy that has escaped you till now.

Surrender Meditation:

Repeat these words aloud as often as you feel is necessary: "By accepting the 'thought' that the world is not the basis of my reality, Perfect Joy is established in my Illumined Mind."

I am that Surrender, now fully Illumined.

The Second Enlightenment, Awakened Heart:

You are being asked to Love the world as God Loves the world, as a reflection of your decisions about yourself. And since the very essence of love is contained within you now, it is the same decision you make about love.

Trust Meditation:

Repeat these words aloud as often as you feel is necessary: "By accepting the 'feeling' that the world is not the basis of my reality, Perfect Joy is established in my Awakened Heart."

I am that Trust now, fully Awakened.

The Third Enlightenment, Realized Soul:

You are being asked to Know what God Knows. How can I describe to you what this is or how you will

Know when you are there? First of all, there is no way you will be able to not recognize this state because it will be so different from everything else you have ever experienced. We can call this the "Peace of God," and it will not escape your attention. It is easy for me to say that you will Know it when you no longer experience separation of any kind, but such a concept is still too hard to appreciate with your mind. It is better to say that you will experience the same reality behind every form, the reality called "The Beloved." When you experience only the Beloved everywhere you look, then you will "Know as God Knows."

Gratitude Meditation:

Repeat these words aloud as often as you feel is necessary: "By accepting the 'Truth' that the world is not the basis of my reality, perfect Joy is established in my Realized Soul."

I am that Gratitude NOW, fully Realized.

— Brother

Lesson Twenty Seven

The Seventh Attribute: Clarity

Who is speaking to you now? We have asked this question before, and you may have already arrived at your decision. We will revisit it again because your answer is of great importance at this stage of your learning. The decision you make about this will be the decision you make about yourself, and that, after all, is all that is ultimately important.

Who is Jeshua and what role do I play in your learning to be an Instrument of Peace? Am I a man with a personality that existed on this earth two thousand years ago, but not now? Where am I now and is it possible for me, or anyone else for that matter, to share my wisdom and energy with those who still claim bodies and form? Is it possible that I have been sharing these lessons with you these many weeks, and that your willingness to accept this creates an opening for you to likewise "be" the same? Or have you accepted this idea more as a story or a concept because the lessons have some value for your life?

Why are these questions so important at this time? It is because you must begin accepting yourself as I am asking you to accept me. I have said many times that you cannot receive any gift that you are not willing to likewise give. Therefore, I am asking you to give me the blessing of your perfection so that we may share it together. I am asking you to see me as your teacher, so that you may teach yourself. Personalities do not matter at all, especially now, so my request is not ultimately related to who you think I was. It is only related to who you know I AM, for then will you know yourself to be the same. We are not separate or divided in any way. We are one, and so is your decision about me. What you decide about me you will decide about yourself. That is why I have come, and it is why you will go to others. I have not come to give life, but to reveal it.

There are many who claim to speak with my voice or to share messages from me. How will you know the difference, when it is real or when it is an illusion? Whoever speaks with the Voice of "Knowing" speaks with my voice. There is no other, for a voice that speaks from a place of "not-knowing" is not heard at all. The voice of "not-knowing" is the voice of the ego that thinks it knows a great deal, but which makes no sense at all except to others' egos. I say that it is not heard because it has no real impact. Why would you want to speak with a voice that makes no impact? That is why you have been called to be a Spiritual Peacemaker, to have an impact in the world. Give up the words and thoughts that mean nothing at all, and speak only with my voice, the "Voice of the Awakened One."

Whenever you speak, speak through and as me. Do not hesitate in this. Know that it is my voice they are hearing, for only then will your message be true. When you KNOW the Truth and speak from that Knowing, then you will perceive no difference between us. Then will your message be clear, for clarity is our next step.

The First Enlightenment, Illumined Mind:

Enlightenment is not something you do, but something you SEE. When you SEE it everywhere then it will be real to you. What you SEE, you are. You are allowing the Light of Truth to penetrate you on three levels, which we are calling the Three Enlightenments. The first step is for your sight to be made clear, for only then will you understand why you are here. Look around, then, and SEE who you are through these others. Then let the same Holy Sight fall upon yourself.

Surrender Meditation:

Repeat these words as often as you feel is necessary: "My mind surrenders control that I may SEE what is real." I do not know what anything means, and therefore I am able to be shown what was once so obscure. I am that Clarity now, fully Illumined.

The Second Enlightenment, Awakened Heart:

Once you are able to SEE what is real, then you can FEEL the same. Enlightenment has now been accepted by your heart, and so are you now awake. As you claim this you will know it to be true. Do not let another second go by without claiming who you are. Why would you want to stay ignorant when the knowledge has come? Why would you stay in a dark room when you feel the Light so close to you? There is no reason for you to remain in this world when a whole new reality has been waiting for you. FEEL this reality and it is yours. I have been feeling it for you, but now you must feel it for yourself.

Trust Meditation:

Repeat these words as often as you feel is necessary: "I am willing to trust the Light, and to Feel as God Feels." I am that Clarity now, fully Awakened.

The Third Enlightenment, Realized Soul:

Now will you Know what God Knows. God knows only one thing: Love. Therefore, you are contained within that Love, that Oneness, for it is your true home. Now perhaps you can see that I have not asked you to leave anything behind, but to simply be where you belong. It is not something you do with your body. It is not something that changes your personality. It is simply something you Realize in your Soul. Open, then, and Know that you are God.

Gratitude Meditation:

Repeat these words as often as you feel is necessary: "I am Grateful for what I Know." I am that Clarity now, fully Realized.

—Brother

Lesson Twenty Eight

The Eighth Attribute: Understanding

In the last lesson we shared this thought: "Everyone that speaks from the place of 'Knowing speaks with my voice, while the place of 'not-knowing' does not exist at all." Herein lies the deepest truth I can offer. When you enter the chamber of your "Self," then there is no difference between us because our voice is the "Voice for God." When you speak on your own, or from the "self" that exists only in your imagination, then you are mute before God. Your holiness is certainly secure, for that cannot change, but your voice and the gift you can offer is forgotten, waiting for you to step back, surrender, and return to the place where God's Voice is yours again.

Does it surprise you when I say that yours is the Voice for God? It is this surprise that keeps you separated from your real function. Know that it is true and it is. Know that your voice speaks for and as God and it will be so. It is not vanity to claim this, as your ego would have you believe. It is vanity to claim that God's will for you can be challenged by your meaningless dreams. Let them go and they are gone, for they are not supported by anything that is real. Let them pass and they return to the land of shadows from where they were created, sleeping again in the barren ground of the world where you hide from your Self. Let your true voice resound so that the whole world may hear the Truth. Only then will the voices of the other enlightened ones rise like a choir before you. Only then will you know that you are not alone, though all is One within.

You are coming to a place where you fully understand this in your mind and heart, and it is then that you will "Know what God Knows." Your Illumined Mind and Awakened Heart have led you thus far, but they cannot pass into the field that transcends all concepts, the place I cannot describe for you, though you are there with me even now. As I said before, Know you are there and you are. Then you will feel my hand as it touches yours, and you will sense the kiss I place upon your holy cheek. You have drawn closer to me than you realize over these last months, since we began this journey together. And I will continue to guide you until you are aware of the Light that enfolds us, making us as one being before the Throne of God. Your desire to be a Spiritual Peacemaker is all that you need, for the desire alone is enough to break down the remaining barriers. I am giving this to you, and so you must continue to give it to others, for you cannot come to me on your own. All your brothers and sisters must come with you, in your mind and in your heart, for nothing can be left behind. I will not abandon you and you must not abandon them. The shower of Grace that falls upon our anointed heads now is like refreshing rain. Drink and know that you are nearly home.

I said that you will soon "Know what God Knows." How will we define this Divine Knowing, that which you will soon claim? Here it is, so simple that you will be unable to pass it by another moment: You are holy beyond measure, and God Loves You. Herein lies your peace, and the peace of all beings.

The First Enlightenment and Meditation, Illumined Mind:

I believe in my Mind that my meaningless dreams cannot change the Holy Will of God. I have given my mind too much power, thinking that the dream it has created is stronger than the reality created for it by God. Open your eyes and understand what you have missed till now. You cannot understand the world while your eyes are closed, and yet this has been the desire of your ego. It prefers ignorance over knowledge. It would

140

rather have you remain helpless than realize that you have all the strength in the Universe. Which will you choose, then, weakness or the strength of God? Choose well, for your brothers and sisters need to follow your example. You are a Spiritual Peacemaker this moment.

The Second Enlightenment and Meditation, Awakened Heart:

I feel in my Heart that my meaningless dreams cannot change the Holy Will of God. Love alone will bring me to the Home where I belong. My heart is now awake, and so I am able to feel what is real. I begin by "Seeing as God Sees," and then I move to the next step of "Feeling as God Feels." God feels only love, and so I give this gift that it may be mine.

The Third Enlightenment and Meditation, Realized Soul:

I know in my Soul that my meaningless dreams cannot change the Holy Will of God. In this Knowing, I become that Holy Will Itself, for nothing has changed since I was created. I am Perfect as God is Perfect, and I am Whole as God is Whole. I proclaim now that "I Am That," and since my knowledge of this Grace is mine only as I give it to others, my soul answers with:

"I Am." Over and over I chant, "I am That, I Am." I call and the Universe responds. The Universe calls and I respond. It is the same. It is the same now and always. "I Am That, I Am." What more is required but this? Where else can I hope to ascend but to the throne where the echo of these words are all I hear? "I Am That, I Am." I will rest now, knowing that my journey is complete. I have not changed the Holy Will of God. I am Home. I am Home. I am Home.

— Brother

Lesson Twenty Nine

The Ninth Attribute: Depth

It is not the depth of this world we are seeking together, but of the world beyond your imagination. Spiritual depth comes from answering one question correctly: "Who am I?" I am the Christ come to save the world from meaningless dreams where sickness and death seem to rule. I am the holy extension of the Mind and Will of God, fulfilling the foresight of the prophets of old. I am all of that, as are you. In fact, I cannot know myself to be any of these things until I know you to be them first. You are the extension of the love and the loveliness of God. I have seen it in you, and I Know that I am the same.

You have given others this gift, but you have not allowed yourself to receive it back. Listen, Beloved Ones, for this lesson will be the cornerstone of all the rest. If you can grasp what I am about to say to you, then you will Know yourself as I know you. Here is what I most long to share:

"Your eyes are already perfect, though they may, for a moment, be covered with scales. Please accept the gift of my Perfect Sight of you, then you will see what is so clear to me. I need you to stand by my side in full awareness. The Universe needs you to walk the path of truth in quiet freedom. You need your Self, and yet you will not fulfill this need until you willingly receive what I offer. Please open now and accept what my hand holds out to you. It is your life. It is your love. This is the moment when you must decide. You are ready NOW!"

Many times throughout this course I have asked you to understand that the world you created, the world of separation and form, is not real. We would do well to discuss this further so that it does not escape our attention. I said that any voice that speaks from the place of "not-knowing" makes no real impact and therefore isn't real. Whatever you do that draws you away from your true purpose here, that of being an Emissary of Light, creates no real impact in the world because it is not eternal. You are eternal, so how can something that is not like you in such a vital way hurt you at all? It cannot. You have forgotten that you are so full of life, and have therefore led yourself to imagine that you are vulnerable and alone. This is the illusion you have created for yourself, and it is the world you chose to see to justify that illusion. But a real impact in eternity it has not, and you are eternal. I do not perceive any of this as a threat, and now I am asking you to do the same. The world you created in your imagination is not the world you really want. This is the gift you can receive today, if only you would finally choose it.

You have called to the Universe and it has answered. You call, as I once did, "I Am That," but the Universe does not respond with the words, "You Are." It responds with the words, "I Am." What does that tell you? When the Universe answers you, it answers as you. It is critically important that you understand this now. I will say it again so you will not miss it: The Universe responds AS you.

When you created your ego you looked out and said, "I Am That," then you looked around for something to identify with. It chose the body and the personality, and therefore could not hear the Universe's Holy Response, for you are far more than you believe yourself to be. You were deaf to its reply and so were not able to complete the cycle. But now you are. Proclaim who you are and live from that proclamation, that is all I am asking of you, and then listen as the Universe responds with the one gift that will set you free. "I Am." And so are all things bound by the Holy Vision of God. You are bound now, for your willingness to accept this has been enough to lay aside all things of time.

Illumined Mind and the Awakened Heart:

Today we will not choose to separate these two enlightenments, but to see them as the same. We have separated them till now only that you may understand them. But now full release is required of all the concepts we have held, especially of separation. And so, for the next four lessons we will look upon this with new eyes, and we will open in a new way.

The instructions will be very simple. For the next three days, look out upon the world you created as it really is. Look at all the things around you, what you perceive as beautiful and what you perceive as ugly, that which you call good and that which you say is bad. As you look upon all these things, say with a whisper or aloud: "I Am That." Know that you are that thing, that person, or that condition. This is not a metaphor. It is the truth that you are now ready to embrace. Then listen for the holy answer that comes from whatever it is you look upon. "I AM!" It is a gift to you, for you are all the things you see around you, even what you have called evil. Embrace it all now. Your willingness to practice this exercise fully will be the measure of your progress.

Realized Soul:

Are you willing to enter into this final stage of your awakening as a Spiritual Peacemaker? If you do this, then you will experience the Truth you have been seeking since you were created. It is my promise, and I will keep it.

—Brother

Lesson Thirty

The Tenth Attribute: Generosity

I am holding your hand firmly in mine. I know that you feel this. You have surrendered and I have come to you, not as a teacher but as a guide. I have walked the path you are walking now. Who else would you want for this Holy Task but one who knows the way? The blind cannot lead the blind, and as long as your eyes remain closed you need someone who has removed the heavy scales that keep the Grace from appearing so near. You are ready to open, and I will be there with you when you do. Let that be your comfort for now, knowing that you will never be abandoned.

We are nearing our journey's end. We have walked this winding path together toward the Home you never left at all, save in your imaginary dreams. God has given you many gifts, but making what isn't real true is not one of them. However, you can make what isn't real "seem" true, and that is what you have done. There is nowhere for you to go but forward, for the path to ignorance has dissolved behind you. We are together now, one Holy Mind communicating with another Holy Mind. Another step and you will Feel what I Feel, and Know what I Know. Then you will understand why I have taken such care to bring you to this Holy Moment. Then you will understand why I love you so.

The statement of truth we have been working with, "I Am That, I Am," is all you need now. I asked you to look around during the day and identify everything you see as "who you are." I Am That tree. I Am That mountain. In doing so you have jumped past the limiting beliefs of the ego and realized that you cannot be identified by anything particular, but by the ALL. Today's lesson takes us a step further, and if you are able to realize what I am aiming to reveal, then you will find yourself where I am, in the Heaven you never left. The next step is so very simple, and yet it will make all the difference if you choose it.

Our goal today is to open our eyes a little wider, to see past the horizon of the ego's design to another reality you have been blind to until now. We will try for the first time to embrace the ALL, to say "I Am That" and have it apply to everything you perceive, not just one particular person or thing. To believe you are some things is no different than thinking you are your body, or the personality that seems to define you. Our goal is to have you open the wings of your Divine Perception so that you may know yourself to be the ALL.

I will stop for a moment so that you can catch your breath. Even with all the mountains we have already climbed together, what I am asking may still seem a distant dream. I ask only one thing, for you to trust me. Suspend your disbelief or hesitation for just a moment and consider that I have a better idea of what you are capable of than you. I look upon the truth in you clearly, while to you it is still in a mist. The mist is beginning to pass, indeed, but we are only at the dawn of your awakening. The sun will surely clear away this mist, but I am able to see past it even now. So give yourself the gift of knowing that you are ready for this step. Then you will move forward in confidence and grace.

Stand in an area where you are comfortable and where you can be alone. Close your eyes and take several deep breaths. Center your Illumined Mind and your Awakened Heart on this thought, breathing deeply as you consider it:

"I am all of this."

Start with your hands extending straight in front of you, hands together. Now open your eyes. As you chant these words over and over, begin to move your hands apart very slowly, and know that your Realized Soul is opening too. Whatever thoughts come into your mind, whatever you see, know that you are that. Whatever person comes to your mind, know that you are that. Open yourself fully to everything that appears before you, and do not push it away. Embrace it all, knowing that they are different aspects of who you are. You will not lose track of the "perceptual being" you have designed by practicing this, so let go of any fear that may arise. You will not lose track of anything that is real, but you may shed all the unreal beliefs you have held till now. This, after all, is your goal and, if you choose, you can achieve it today.

Illumined Mind and Awakened Heart:

We will consider these as one, for so they are. You are nearly awake, and so I will not treat you any differently than how I wish to be treated. What I have offered to you today is the essence of what I am calling "Generosity," for it is what I mean when I say, "Give everything to have everything." I am asking you to open your mind and heart fully so that your blessings may extend to all that is real. There is nothing left for you to do. It is the only thing there ever was for you to do. Now I'm asking you to stand by me and do as I do, for it is the only way you will be called a "Spiritual Peacemaker." Trust me when I say that you are ready for this.

Realized Soul:

There is nothing left for me to give you. You only need follow my final instructions and you will see for yourself. Open your eyes and Know that we are One.

—Brother

Lesson Thirty One

The Eleventh Attribute: Abundance

Your goal today is to seek after what you really want; for that is the only way you will have it. It would seem that you would not need to question this, that you would always be seeking to draw to yourself that which serves and blesses you and your mission. But as you have seen through your own life, this is not always true. There is a part of each one of us that seeks gifts that are not ours, so we find ourselves lost upon roads where we do not belong. Yet even this can be used by the One who is with you now, leading you from darkness into the Light, but only if you have enough courage to uncover the reasons you chose these things in the first place. This is where we will begin our inquiry, and it is what will lead you into the spiritual abundance you seek.

We have addressed these issues before, but now that we are near the end of our course on Spiritual Peacemaking, we will examine them once again so there is no confusion at all. Before you can be clear about what you are, you must also be clear about what you are not. This would not be required if you did not confuse these two in the past, but such is the condition of your life here. The ego's role is to seek but never find. Then you wonder why the world leaves you so unsatisfied. Your Realized Soul does not seek at all, for it KNOWS that all things are already contained there. Nothing is required because nothing is absent. This, of course, is the essence of abundance, while the desire to seek after anything is its denial.

Once again, your Spirit does not seek at all, for it realizes that it is already full. Understand this and your journey will be over. You have been looking outside yourself for what does not exist, and have then been surprised when you were unable to achieve your goal. Time and time again you have done this, all because you have been listening to the wrong voice within, the voice that would have you forget rather than the one that would have you remember. But as always, the Spirit of Truth never closes its wings to you, and you are always given the chance to "Choose Again." Will this be the moment that you decide to lay aside all the things that have not served your life, only your death? If you do, then you will realize the reason you were born into this world, to heal and to bless. That is why you have embarked on this journey with me, but I have nearly led you as far as I can. The next step belongs to you. Will you choose to open your eyes and look upon the love I have revealed, or will you retreat again into the shadowy figures that have taught you nothing except loss? The choice is yours, and you must make it now. That, after all, is the only moment there is for you to choose anything at all.

Know that I am challenging you because I want you to have what you deserve, not be denied anything that is real. I have led you to the edge of a cliff, and it may seem to you that something will be lost if you take this final step. I may tell you that you will be safe, and remind you that I too have suffered through this and taken the step you must now take. But your trust in me must be strong, and I know it is. Are you willing to risk nothing in order to have everything? Read that last sentence again. Are you willing to risk NOTHING in order to have EVERYTHING? This, as unusual as it may seem, is the choice that you must make. Unfortunately, you have not seen it this way until now, otherwise you would have made the choice of life. But that is why you are here, and it is why I am with you. All the lessons we have shared have led to this moment. If you are able to take this final step you will be supported upon the wings of angels and they will guide you to the home your soul longs to return to. You can see it in the distance. Of this I am sure, for I can see it reflecting in your eyes as I speak to you, Beloved. But you must KNOW that my words mean life, otherwise you will interpret them according to the thoughts of death you have held. Open your wings and fly with me. We will be there before you realize anything has happened at all. I will not let you fall, for such a thing is impossible now.

Illumined Mind and Awakened Heart:

(Repeat these words with conviction)

"I have accepted in my mind that I must give everything to have everything, and my heart has felt the approach of this great gift. Now I act upon what I have learned, for my acceptance is not enough. I must complete the cycle of giving and receiving in order to know that I am abundant now. I will not measure this by the standards of the world, but by God's standards. God's currency is love, and so I give this to all that it may be mine. Nothing else will satisfy me now. I give only what I want to receive and, in doing so, see the same gift return to me."

Realized Soul:

"I am standing at the edge of a cliff, and my guide is beside me holding my hand. I will not hesitate in taking the step that leads to the life I seek. I can see my Gentle Home in the distance and I will not wait another moment. I step out with confidence, then fly."

—Brother

Lesson Thirty Two

The Twelfth Attribute: Agape

To Love as God Loves.

You have been told that it is impossible to understand and realize the Love of God. I am telling you now that this should be your only goal. It is the goal of anyone who seeks to be a Spiritual Peacemaker, for what can this Love be but the extension of the peace that surpasses the world of separation and form? It is true that it is impossible to realize the Love of God so long as you cling to conflict of any kind, and yet conflict is the foundation of the world you constructed in your imagination. It is a place of war, and the experience you are seeking is not here. Therefore, the Peace of God can only be found in the world where you really live, the Home you never left. I have said that I am with you there now, and I am waiting for you to open your spiritual eyes and realize this. I want to emphasize this again because it will make this final step, which is the only true step you must make, easily accomplished. Take a deep breath, for you are very near the end of our journey together. Your freedom from despair is a single thought away. Open your eyes and you will see me, and you will know that the Love of God is already yours.

Does it surprise you when I say that realizing the Love of God, Agape, has been your only goal from the beginning? This is because the larger Self which I look upon now, and which you will soon see, has never been threatened by the impossible dream you have tried to construct in place of reality. The question then is, why are you here at all? If your agenda and Holy Spirit's have always been perfectly aligned, then why have you lingered here so long? The answer I am about to give you will not make sense to your mind, but if you allow yourself to dive to the deeper ocean where I have been leading you, then it will make perfect sense to you. Then will you grasp with your heart what even your Illumined Mind cannot comprehend.

Why have you lingered here so long?

"You haven't."

This is how I perceive it now, though I must say that it has not always been so. I am an effective guide because I am able to remember the amnesia that still grips you, though I can see the memory of love beginning to flicker in your mind. I was able to SEE what has never changed. I saw it in others, and that is

159

how I was able to have it myself. I saw my own enlightened mind everywhere, in everyone, and so it was mine. The illusions that once clouded my heart were swept away in an instant, and all things became clear. It was at that instant that I realized the Love of God was my only goal, even while I slept. And that is why I am saying this to you, Beloved, for we have progressed enough now that this gentle memory will easily fall into place within your mind. Every path has led to the Holy Altar you are now about to regain. Know that my words are true, and follow the path I have blazed for you. Then you will realize the completion of your deepest dream.

Illumined Mind and Awakened Heart

Though the world you created in your imagination is not real, you will not "BECOME" the Real World until you fully accept yourself here. The world you look upon is not real, but YOU ARE. Once again, take these words into your Awakened Heart, that you may understand what I am trying to communicate. Even when you are dreaming, YOU ARE REAL WITHIN THE DREAM. Do you understand? When you look about the world you created and say, "I Am That," then you realize that the dream and the dreamer

160

are the same. This is the magic of seeing your own holiness in everything you perceive. It is like stepping closer to your own heart, and your soul will surely follow.

Look upon the world one final time, everything that appears before you both animate and inanimate, and say with love, "I Am That." God's love flows through you and everything you perceive. In other words, God loves you as much when you're asleep as when you're awake. When you learn to imitate this by giving the same gift to others, first in your Illumined Mind and then in your Awakened Heart, then you will have achieved the final attribute. You will suddenly "Love as God Loves," and Agape will flow though everything you do.

Realized Soul

When you are finally able to love in the way I have described, then you will realize the greatest mystery of all, and you will at last be able to call yourself a Spiritual Peacemaker. There is no difference at all between the world you created and the world God created, when Agape is revealed. You are real within both, and so is your love. It is the bridge that leads from one into the other, and is what the mystics described when they said: "Be in the world, but not of the world." I do not want you to go anywhere, for leaving the world was never our goal. I want you to be here fully present and realized. Stand upon the bridge and look upon what you have created, then look upon the world prepared for you by God. When you love as God, they will appear the same, for love will be reflected everywhere you look. What else can Heaven be but this? And where else will you find it but where you are now?

Spend as much time as you can meditating upon the Emissary Wheel in the next three days. The final lesson will be your graduation.

—Brother

Lesson Thirty Three

Do not think that you have finally gained my confidence, for such a thing is impossible. You cannot gain something that you have never lost. Believe, rather, that you have gained your own confidence. That has been the only real goal of this course, the only thing that you have lacked which has kept you from being the Spiritual Peacemaker I perceive. You were not able to look upon the beauty and completion that I see in you, and so you have limited your ability to accept and then give the same. It is like a whole world has passed by us now. You are not the same person that started this course 99 days ago, and yet nothing has changed at all. God's love is the same as it has ever been, regardless of anything you have seemed to do to diminish it. You are still as God created you, and you are at last ready to embrace yourself as I have always embraced you.

And perhaps you are also ready to embrace me, and to have confidence in my confidence in you. In limiting yourself you have also limited me, for it is impossible for us to be separated. I have told you that you are Holy, and yet you were unable to trust me. But now you are, and everything has changed. My confidence in you is complete, and we are now able to leave the world behind and enter fully into the Heaven created for us before time began. I have been waiting for you and now you are here, in full awareness and consciousness. Open your eyes now, and see what you have hidden from until now. Love is all around you.

In the first lesson I told you that you are ready for this shift. Now I tell you that the shift is complete. I am not willing to accept any question about this. There is no longer any room for vacillation, for you have come too far to deny what you have gained. Now you must deny the denial that has plagued you till now. You have been willing to give me the confidence that is required to join our intent as one, and now it is done. I see you as I see myself, as fully enlightened. Now you must do the same. See it in me this moment, and know that it is your own face you look upon. Nothing else is possible now. Accept what is real, and know that you have arrived at your Home.

Look upon the Emissary Wheel again and let your eyes move from one spoke to another. Your vision knows where to go. How else would you have been able to find me, and to discover your Self? Move from point to point and remember all the attributes you have embraced. You have become each one of these. That does not mean that you will never need to be reminded again, just as your former inability to realize your enlightenment hasn't changed anything that is real. The whole tree is contained within the seed, and so are you complete this moment. I will not allow you any further movement from this, for that is my role as a teacher of God. And you will no longer allow any vacillation in yourself, for you are ready to stand beside me. Do you see how easily you regain Heaven? It has always been yours, and so it is easy to return. Bless this day, Beloved, for your homecoming is felt through the whole Universe.

And now, as you continue to gaze upon the wheel, let your eyes focus upon the center circle. This is the place within you that does not move, the Holy Child of God that has never been abandoned by eternity. This is where our time together has led you, to this solid ground where your enlightenment illumines all other minds. Once again, I will not allow any debate in this, for I assure you I am correct. Now that you have attained this level, more will be expected of you, for you are now poised to heal as an enlightened being heals. Your Illumined Mind and Awakened Heart extend as a blessing to all beings, and you serve as you were born to serve. What other gift can you offer now but that which you have received? I have given to you and now you give the same. The peace that flows from you proves that time has no solution for itself. Only eternity can answer what is eternal. So you are now and will always be.

Graduation

This is the moment you have been prepared for. There are times when your heart needs to hear and to know how far you have come. I have said this many times before and I will repeat it once again: You have not gone anywhere at all, but in your consciousness there is no way for us to measure your progress. You stand upon a Holy Bridge from where you will translate the gifts you have received into gifts you give. They will not come in words, but in the Presence that transcends words. But first you must hear from me the words that will finally activate it all. It is my greatest joy now to offer them to you.

YOU ARE AN ENLIGHTENED BEING, FULLY REALIZED.

Do you believe that I have offered every word you have read in this course? If you do, then you must also trust that the commission I have given is true. You are an Enlightened Being sent to bless all beings. You are no longer ready. You are there. Love is complete within you, and your heart is no longer split off from your Holy Mind. It is done! It is done! It is done!

I still have so much more to say that will make this reality solid within you. Continue to walk with me.

—Brother

Conclusion

Read the words at the end of the last lessons once again: "YOU ARE AN ENLIGHTENED BEING, FULLY REALIZED." Do you believe it's true? Can you sense a shift in your consciousness that reveals the changeless reality of your Awakened Self? Perhaps it's subtle and difficult to perceive. Even if it is, are you willing to accept that the Truth is forever True, that this Truth is in you now? If you are, then you're ready to step into a new function, one that was given to you before time began — the function of being a savior in this world. You're finally able to See through the facade to the Holy City you never left accept in your imagination. And you're able to see all your brothers and sisters there as well, the Heaven that is forever Whole in your Sacred Mind.

Step forward with confidence now. Nothing can be added to the gift you've finally received. There is no other book and no other teacher that can give you more than EVERYTHING, but to realize this you must first understand that you HAVE everything. Nothing can be added and nothing can be taken away. The only thing that's changed is your willingness to fully receive your birthright, the gift of perfection that has always been yours. But never forget that you must strive to be the source of that gift since that's the only way you'll stay awake. Withhold the gift of perfection and you'll fall once again into the world of dreams. But if you give that which has been so generously given to you, you'll lift free from this world and ascend to the Home that has waited for you since time began.

You have received the 33 lessons that Jeshua gave at the Dead Sea many years ago, and they are just as relevant today. They are some of the same lessons he offered his closest friends 2000 years ago, and they have been offered to you now. All you have to do is fully accept them and salvation is yours. The moment of your awakening is complete. Welcome home, Beloved, welcome home.

An Invitation ~

The Enlightenment Partnership Program:

These 33 lessons are the equivalent of Jeshua taking you by the hand and leading you into the Light. Can you think of anything more amazing? But there are still times when we need a mighty companion to accompany us on this journey, helping us remove the final blocks to the awareness of love. That is what the Enlightenment Partnership program designed for, a way to continue your journey of awakening, accompanied by one who has already walked the path that leads to Heaven.

Imagine having James Twyman walking beside you on this journey. The Enlightenment Partnership coaching program is a three month deep dive that will help you finally break free. During the three month program you'll be in contact with James every day, through text messages, phone calls, emails and a weekly Zoom call. You'll have full access to a brother who is fully dedicated to your awakening and who gives himself completely to walking you home.

To receive more information on the program go to www.JamesFTwyman.com. You can even schedule a free 10 minute long call with James to ask questions and see if the program is for you. Take the time to check it out.

About the Author

James F. Twyman is an Episcopal/Anglican priest and a Franciscan brother in The Community of Francis and Clare. He has written 19 books including the NY Times bestseller The Moses Code, has directed or produced seven feature films including the award winning Redwood Highway and Indigo, and has recorded nearly 20 music CDs. Known internationally as The Peace Troubadour, James has traveled to countries at war to perform The Peace Concert for over 25 years. During many of these peace journeys he called people from around the world to pray and meditate for peace during World Synchronized Meditations. In some cases millions of people participated in these meditations. James is also the founder and spiritual leader of Namaste Village, a nondual interfaith community in Ajijic, Mexico. For more information on Namaste Village go to www.Namaste-Village.com.

Made in United States
Orlando, FL
13 February 2023

29980177R00109